The Student/The College/The Law

The Student/The College/The Law

WILLIAM T. O'HARA

JOHN G. HILL, JR.

Teachers College Press

Teachers College, Columbia University
New York and London

For
Barbara S. O'Hara
and
Barbara O. Hill

PREFACE

Preparation of *The Student/The College/The Law* began during the campus turbulence of the late 1960's. Student involvement in the conflict and turmoil of that period suggested the need for a book that would clearly define the law bearing upon the relationship of students and institutions of higher education. Few sources dealing with this area were available, and most did not provide comprehensive, up-to-date treatment. In fact, the courts prior to the 1960's gave little attention to the subject. A limited number of decisions had been rendered, and the large majority supported the privileged position of the college or university. With 1964 and the outburst of campus dissent, it became apparent that students were no longer willing to accept the old rule. Mario Savio and the "Free Speech Movement" at Berkeley were the vanguard of a new college age in the United States. As the first of the post-World War II babies to attend college, these students were articulate, intelligent, and bent on obtaining the right of self-determination in matters affecting their campus life. Their awareness and independence as individuals dictated a special interest in the legal rights of students.

Although campuses, in a relative sense, are quieter today, this same interest continues. From the frustrations and disappointments of Berkeley, Kent State, and Jackson State and hundreds of other unresolved campus confrontations, there has developed a recognition that our legal system is a major force for change—to be used rather than ignored or opposed. Instead of invading and occupying an administrator's office, students now see the long-term and more lasting benefits of seeking recourse for wrongs through mediation and courts of law. Student curiosity in the legal process is widespread. The degree of student eagerness to know their rights and to exercise them is unprecedented in the history of American higher education. This book is intended to respond to this student interest. It provides a comprehensive review of the leading cases that have a bearing upon the college student and his life on campus. Every attempt has been made to simplify the presentation of the legal principles to facilitate the layman's understanding. Selected cases are presented at the end of each chapter to provide the reader with an opportunity to examine the text of leading court decisions. The cases will reveal the process of reasoning gone into by the courts in arriving at their final judgments. Furthermore, the reader will gain a greater appreciation of the methods used in reaching a judicial determination.

It is appropriate to close with a word of caution. This book presents the most recent cases handed down by the courts on the legal rights of college students. The law is in constant flux, however, and any subsequent single decision can seriously alter a legal rule applied to any given circumstances. The reader should be ever mindful of this fact in drawing parallels from the book to current campus situations.

Finally, in considering the law and its relationship to the college student, the volume traces the area's historical development, its current status, and its possible future growth. In no event is it a substitute for the expert advice of an attorney. Any person who feels that he has a legal cause of action should never fail to seek the professional assistance of a competent lawyer.

W. T. O'H.
J. G. H.

September 1972

ACKNOWLEDGMENTS

The authors wish to acknowledge the assistance and encouragement of several persons who participated in the preparation of *The Student/ The College/The Law*. The initial encouragement of Robert McKay, Dean of the New York University Law School, is deeply appreciated. The support of The University of Connecticut Research Foundation proved to be a vital factor in the completion of our research, and we are indebted to it. The assistance of Attorneys Richard Gitlin, Bonnie Myrun Milstein, and Wendy Susco is gratefully acknowledged. The library reference work of Judith Lahey, Helen Petty, and Rose York was invaluable, and the clerical help of Beverly Anderson, Maxine Frank, Patricia Gall, Joyce Gatonska, and Lynn Quibble contributed substantially to our efforts.

Finally, special appreciation is extended to a law student, Patricia Mulkeen, and to Mr. O'Hara's secretary, Elizabeth DeNoia. Both made important contributions to our research and the preparation of the manuscript.

CONTENTS

The Student/The College/The Law

1

ADMISSIONS

The decision of a college to accept or reject an applicant for admission is one of far-reaching consequences. It is a matter that involves serious questions of a legal nature with which students should be familiar.

One must keep in mind that until recently a college education, whether received at a public or a private institution, was considered a privilege granted to the student, and courts based their decisions concerning admissions policies on this theory. A question certain to confront the courts in the future is the validity of this theory, especially as applied to public institutions of higher learning. If the theory of higher education as a citizen's right prevails, then cases decided on the "privilege" standard will no longer be compelling authority. If such a shift does come, its consequences no doubt will be seen first in the public sector of higher education. Breakthroughs in the admissions policies of private institutions may follow, especially if federal and state aid help to support these schools.

PUBLIC INSTITUTIONS

Differences are frequently apparent between the present admissions policies of public and of private universities. These differences exist in part because the courts recognize that admission, although not a right, is a privilege provided for and protected by laws of each state.

In private institutions, however, admission is based on the more exclusive contract theory, which means that the school may choose with whom it wishes to contract. The private institution can be as selective as it wishes and can refuse applicants for reasons other than their inadequate academic preparation or the institution's space limitations. Thus, courts have so far upheld a private university's right to discriminate on the basis of race, religion, or sex.[1]

Entrance requirements may be established to demand a certain academic level from each applicant, to limit enrollment to coincide with the capacity of campus facilities, or for other legitimate reasons. As a general rule, however, public institutions must establish requirements for admission that are reasonable and that can be applied in a non-arbitrary manner.[2]

The power to set admissions standards at public universities is vested in the state legislatures, who, in turn, may delegate the responsibility to state Boards of Trustees or Regents. The principle that a state legislature has the power to create such rules for its public university with no supervision or interference by the courts was emphasized by the Supreme Court of Mississippi in *Board of Trustees of University of Mississippi v. Waugh.*[3] In that case, the court refused to accept the student-plaintiff's argument that the Fourteenth Amendment of the United States Constitution prohibited the state Board's enforcing a regulation that denied admission to anyone who refused to sign an anti-fraternity pledge. The court recognized the Board's rule-making power and held that since the right to attend the educational institutions of the state was not a natural right but a "gift of civilization," the student could not refuse to obey the regulation. The courts leave it to the discretion of University officials to decide what is "reasonable and not arbitrary" and, unless a plaintiff can show evidence of clear abuse of that discretion, the courts will not interfere. In the case of *Lesser v. Board of Education of the City of New York,*[4] the plaintiff contended that the decision of Brooklyn College

---

[1]15 *American Jurisprudence* 2d Colleges and Universities § 17 (Rochester, N.Y.: The Lawyers' Co-operative Publishing Co., 1964).

[2]George M. Johnson, *Education Law*, p. 89 (East Lansing: Michigan State University Press, 1969).

[3]105 Miss. 623, 633 (1913); affirmed 237 U.S. 589 (1915).

[4]18 A.D.2d 388 (1963) New York.

in rejecting her son's application as a non-tuition paying student was arbitrary. But the Appellate Division of the state's Supreme Court refused to review the college's decision and ruled that:

A court should refrain from interjecting its views within those delicate areas of school administration which relate to the eligibility of applicants . . . unless . . . a practice of discrimination or gross error has been shown. . . . The judicial task ends when it is found that the applicant has received from the college authorities uniform treatment under reasonable regulations fairly administered.[5]

Mrs. Lesser objected not to the academic requirements for admission, but to the fact that the authorities refused to bend them to admit her son. The court refused to come to her aid.

But the courts *will* review the reasonableness of certain admissions policies established by state universities if a student can show that he is being discriminated against by the regulations. Accordingly, Boards of Trustees acting as agents of the respective states are prohibited by the Fourteenth Amendment from discriminating on the basis of race when implementing admissions policies. As applied to public education by the decision in *Brown v. Board of Education of Topeka*,[6] the amendment's equal protection clause prohibits segregation by race. Prior to that decision, more then twenty states had laws permitting the practice.[7] But sixteen years prior to the Brown decision, the United States Supreme Court, in *Missouri ex rel. Gaines v. Canada, Registrar of the University of Missouri*,[8] had placed a limit on the "separate but equal" doctrine as advanced by *Plessy v. Ferguson*[9] by refusing to allow its application in admissions policies of institutions of higher learning.

The applicability of the *Brown* decision to public higher education was specifically affirmed by the Supreme Court in a case

---

[5]*Ibid.*, at 391.

[6]347 U.S. 483 (1954), 349 U.S. 294 (1955).

[7]Arthur E. Sutherland, "Segregation by Race In Public Schools, Retrospect and Prospect Law and Contemporary Problems." 20 *Duke University School of Law* 1 (1955). The states were: (mandatory) Alabama, Arkansas, Delaware, Florida, Georgia, Kentucky, Louisiana, Maryland, Mississippi, Missouri, North Carolina, Oklahoma, South Carolina, Tennessee, Texas, Virginia, West Virginia, and the District of Columbia; (optional) Arizona, Kansas, New Mexico, and Wyoming.

[8]305 U.S. 337 (1938).

[9]163 U.S. 537 (1896).

involving the University of North Carolina.[10] On May 23, 1955, in
the wake of the *Brown* decision, the Board of Trustees of the University resolved to deny admission to members of the Negro race. But in
a suit brought be Negro applicants against the Board, the United
States District Court held that Negroes as a class could not be excluded from the University solely because of their race. The court
suggested that the *Brown* prohibition of separate educational facilities
as inherently unequal applies with greater force to students at the
college-university level. It observed:

> Indeed it is fair to say that [this prohibition] applies with greater force to
> students . . . in the concluding years of their formal education as they are
> about to engage in the serious business of adult life.[11]

At the same time, the court took pains to point out that the Board
of Trustees retained the power to establish other qualifications for
admission.

Selective admission policies based on race are defunct, a short-
sighted practice well laid to rest. Today, in a more enlightened era,
unprecedented efforts are being made in public and even private
institutions to bring minority racial groups into the mainstream of
collegiate life. Although these efforts represent positive progress, they
have not eliminated the controversial nature of the subject.

Recently, the Supreme Court of the State of Washington handed
down a decision that is potentially of great significance. In the case,
a rejected law school applicant of the Caucasian race challenged the
right of the University of Washington Law School to reject qualified
applicants and to accept less qualified applicants because of their
minority status. The court's ruling found the law school's admission
policy favoring minority groups to be unlawful and ordered the
plaintiff's admission. The judge's reasoning recognized that *Brown*
had decided that public education must be equally available to all
regardless of race. The opinion went on to say:

> After that decision the Fourteenth Amendment could no longer be
> stretched to accommodate the needs of any race. Policies of discrimination

---

[10]*Frasier v. Board of Trustees of University of North Carolina*, 134 F. Supp. 589 (1955)
(M.D. North Carolina); affirmed 350 U.S. 979 (1956).

[11]*Ibid.*, at 592.

will inevitably lead to reprisals. In my opinion, the only safe rule is to treat all races alike, and I feel that is what is required under the equal protection clause.[12]

There is no doubt that this case will be appealed, and it is not inconceivable that it will eventually be heard by the United States Supreme Court. The issue is one that could have tremendous impact.

Another area of discrimination that, until recent times, has not been questioned on any wide scale presents the question: Can women be excluded from public colleges or universities on the basis of sex? The Texas Court of Civil Appeals decided affirmatively in *Heaton v. Bristol.*[13] The Agricultural and Mechanical College of Texas, to which females were denied admission, offered courses in seventeen majors not available at other state institutions, including Texas Women's College. Nevertheless, the court held that, viewed as a whole, the state educational system, comprising sixteen co-educational, one all-male, and one all-female, institutions, did not discriminate, but made ample provisions for the education of both sexes. A South Carolina case has reached a similar conclusion,[14] although, in that case, men attempted to obtain admission to an all-female college.

The law is not settled on this point, however. In *Kirstein v. The Rector and Visitor of the University of Virginia,*[15] a federal district court reached a different conclusion. It found that denial of admission based on sex constituted discrimination as prohibited by the Fourteenth Amendment. The decision made it apparent that a state may not deny to women, on the basis of sex, educational opportunities at its state university.

The outcome of this question remains to be settled. The movement of single-sex colleges toward co-educational status may make the issue moot, or federal legislation may prohibit discrimination on

---

[12]*DeFunis v. Odegaard*, No. 741727, Superior Court of the State of Washington, September 22, 1971. Case on appeal to the Supreme Court of the State of Washington, No. 42198. A different conclusion was reached in *Maise v. Board of Regents of the University of Colorado*, Civil Action No. C-3111, United States District Court for the District of Colorado, August 9, 1971.

[13]317 S.W. 2d 86 (Texas, 1958). Rehearing denied 1958.

[14]*Williams v. McNair*, 316 F. Supp. 134 (1970).

[15]309 F. Supp. 184 (1970).

the basis of sex.[16] In any event, it is certain that admission barriers or quotas based on the sex of the applicant will not be passively accepted and remain unchallenged as they have in the past.

If a state may not discriminate on the basis of race or sex by the admissions policies of its public universities, may such a state discriminate on the basis of residence? That is, may an institution deny admission or scholarship aid to non-residents? The question was raised in a suit instituted by the American Commuters Association, a New Jersey corporation of some 1800 members.[17] As non-resident taxpayers, the members challenged the constitutionality of New York's Education Law 6301, which conferred state educational benefits on resident taxpayers only. The petitioners pointed out that as non-resident commuters who earned almost all their income in New York, they paid the same rate of taxes as residents and should, therefore, receive the same benefits.

The Federal District Court for the Southern District of New York denied the Association's claim and recognized the right of a municipality or a state to limit admission to its educational institutions on the basis of residence alone. This decision has special significance at a time when many legislatures have enacted, or are contemplating action on, regulations limiting non-resident enrollment at state institutions of higher education. Clearly, a state does have the prerogative to establish such limitations.

---

[16]H.R. 5191 and H.R. 7248, 92nd Cong., 1st Sess. (1971). Section 1001 of H.R. 5191 reads:

(a) No person in the United States shall, on the ground of sex, be discriminated against by a recipient of Federal financial assistance for any education program or activity. The preceding sentence shall not, however, preclude differential treatment based upon sex where sex is a bona fide ground for such differential treatment.

(b) No recipient of Federal financial assistance for an education program or activity shall, because of an individual's sex—

(1) discharge that individual, fail or refuse to hire (except in instances where sex is a bona fide occupational qualification) that individual, or otherwise discriminate against him or her with respect to compensation, terms, conditions, or privileges of employment; or

(2) limit, segregate, or classify employees in any way which would deprive or tend to deprive that individual of employment opportunities or otherwise adversely affect his or her status as an employee.

[17]*American Commuters Association v. Levitt*, 279 F. Supp. 40 (1967).

PRIVATE INSTITUTIONS

Court decisions to this date have refused to apply the same guidelines regarding discrimination in policies of public colleges and universities to the admissions policies of private institutions. Under the contract theory, even a student who meets an institution's admission requirements has no legal right to admission. The contract theory recognizes that a private institution has the right to accept or to reject any applicant without justifying its action. Nor can such a college or university be compelled to accept an applicant, regardless of the basis of its decision. The only limitations on its admission policies are those contained in its charter as granted by the state.

The leading case in this area is *People ex rel. Tinkoff v. Northwestern University*,[18] in which a rejected applicant brought suit to compel the private institution to admit him. The court refused to accept the plaintiff's contention that the university served the public interest and held that no reason need be given when an application is rejected.

As early as 1909, the courts determined that private colleges have the exclusive authority to determine who shall be admitted. In *Booker v. Grand Rapids Medical College*,[19] the Supreme Court of Michigan observed:

Private institutions of learning, though incorporated, may select those whom they will receive, and may discriminate by sex, age, proficiency in learning and otherwise.[20]

The court, in refusing relief to the Negro students, who had been denied admission solely on the basis of their race, pointed out that Michigan law imposed no public duty on private institutions to admit any and all students, but rather allows them to select students and to discriminate on whatever basis they deem suitable.

A case decided much later arrived at a similar conclusion. In *Reed v. Hollywood Professional School*,[21] a five-year-old Negro was denied

[18]333 Ill. App. 224 (1947). Rehearing denied 1948.
[19]156 Mich. 95 (1909).
[20]*Ibid.*, at 99.
[21]169 Cal. App.2d 887 (1959) and 338 P.2d 633 (Calif. 1959).

admission to the Hollywood Professional School. The Superior Court, Appellate Department, ruled that a private school is not a place of "public accommodation" and hence is not subject to the provisions of the California Civil Rights Act.[22] It further commented that the ultimate question of whether a person may be denied admission to a private school on the basis of race must be decided in part on the distinction between public and private education. Although the court acknowledged that, according to *Brown v. Board of Education of Topeka*, racial discrimination in public education is unconstitutional, it maintained that "private schools should be entitled to contract or refuse to contract with students of their choice for whatever reason."[23]

Private institutions can establish such standards as they wish, academic or otherwise, to determine the admissibility of students. But, as suggested earlier, the right of non-public schools to set criteria for admission may be affected as these institutions receive greater state or federal support. To the extent that they become "state agents" for the handling of such funds, they come "within the constitutional and statutory proscription against discrimination on the basis of race or color."[24] But for now it can safely be said that the private sector of higher education is free to choose whom it wishes to admit.

CONCLUSION

The outcome of legal questions related to college admission often depends upon the public or private nature of the institution. The opportunity to attend a public college or university is considered a privilege. It is not a right. The criteria and selection process for admitting students, however, must be reasonable and not arbitrary, and consistent with constitutional principles.

On the other hand, private colleges and universities face no such requirements. Admission can be made on any basis the institution wishes to establish. Conversely, candidates can be rejected on the basis of color, race, or religion, or for any other reason.

[22]Cal. Civil Code SS51, 52 (West, 1954).
[23]338 P.2d 637.
[24]*Ibid.*, at 637.

Whether the private sector will be able to continue this practice without the courts' placing some restraint upon it is difficult to determine. Increased amounts of federal and state aid to private colleges and universities might be a determining factor in changing the status of these institutions. It is not inconceivable that the courts will view them as sufficiently public to require a stricter adherence to constitutional principles in making admission decisions.[25] If the step is in that direction, the *Model Code for Student Rights, Responsibilities, and Conduct* offers a sensible approach:

Access to Higher Education: Within the limits of its facilities, the institution shall be open to all applicants who are qualified according to its admission requirements.

A. The institution shall make clear the characteristics and expectations of students which it considers relevant to its programs.

B. Under no circumstances may an applicant be denied admission because of race or ethnic background.

C. (Optional) Religious preference for applicants shall be clearly and publicly stated.[26]

[25]The case of *Ryan v. Hofstra University*, 324 N.Y.S.2d 964 (1971) lends credence to this theory.

[26]*Model Code for Student Rights, Responsibilities, and Conduct*, prepared by the Committee on Student Rights and Responsibilities, Law Student Division, American Bar Association (Chicago: American Bar Association, 1969), p. 1.

Frasier v. Board of Trustees of The
University of North Carolina et al.
United States District Court, M.D. North Carolina, 1955
134 F. Supp. 589.

SOPER, Circuit Judge:

This suit seeks a declaratory judgment that certain orders of the Board of Trustees of the Consolidated University of North Carolina, which deny admission to the undergraduate schools of the institution to members of the Negro race, are in violation of the equal protection clause of the 14th Amendment of the Constitution of the United States. The plaintiffs also ask for an injunction restraining the University and its trustees and officers from denying admission to the undergraduate schools to Negroes solely because of their race and color. . . .

The plaintiffs are three Negro youths who are citizens and residents of North Carolina and graduates of the Hillside High School of Durham, which is accredited by the Southern Association of Secondary Schools and Colleges and by the State Department of Public Instruction of the State. The plaintiffs made formal application for admission to the undergraduate school of the University on April 19, 1955, and accompanied their application with a record of their academic achievements, character and personal references, as required by the rules of the University. On April 27, 1955, they received identical letters from the Director of Admissions in which they were told that the Trustees of the University had not changed the policy of admission of Negroes who were eligible to make application for graduate and professional studies not offered at a Negro college in the state, but were not eligible at that time to apply for admission to the undergraduate schools. Thereupon the plaintiffs requested the University to reverse its policy of discrimination against Negroes and the Board of Trustees in reply, on May 23, 1955, reaffirmed its policy by passing the following resolution:

The State of North Carolina having spent millions of dollars in providing adequate and equal educational facilities in the undergraduate departments of its institutions of higher learning for all races, it is hereby declared to be the policy of the Board of Trustees of the Consolidated University of North Carolina that applications of Negroes to the undergraduate schools of the three branches of the Consolidated University be not accepted. . . .

It will have been noticed that the resolution of the Board of May 23, 1955, excluding Negroes from the undergraduate schools of the University, was promulgated after the decision of the Supreme Court in *Brown v. Board of Education of Topeka, Kansas*, 347 U.S. 483. In that case on May 17, 1954, the Supreme Court held that "in the field of public education the doctrine of 'separate but equal' has no place," and that the segregation of white and Negro children in the public schools of a State solely on the basis of race denies to Negro children the equal protection of the laws guaranteed by the 14th Amendment.

The only answer to this far reaching decision, and the only defense on the merits of the cases offered by the defendants in this suit is that the Supreme Court in *Brown v. Board of Education of Topeka, Kansas*, decided that segregation of the races was prohibited by the 14th Amendment only in respect to the lower public schools and did not decide that the separation of the races in schools on the college and university level is unlawful. We think that the contention is without merit. That the decision of the Supreme Court was limited to the facts before it is true, but the reasoning on which the decision was based is as applicable to schools for higher education as to schools on the lower level. Chief Justice Warren, speaking for the Court, said:

Today, education is perhaps the most important function of state and local governments. Compulsory school attendance laws and the great expenditures for education both demonstrate our recognition of the importance of education to our democratic society. It is required in the performance of our most basic public responsibilities, even service in the armed forces. It is the very foundation of good citizenship. Today it is a principal instrument in awakening the child to cultural values, in preparing him for later professional training, and in helping him to adjust normally to his environment. In these days, it is doubtful that any child may reasonably be expected to succeed in life if he is denied the opportunity of an education. Such an opportunity, where the state has undertaken to provide it, is a right which must be made available to all on equal terms.

Again, quoting from the decision in the *Kansas* case, he said:

Segregation of white and colored children in public schools has a detrimental effect upon the colored children. The impact is greater when it has the sanction of the law; for the policy of separating the races is usually interpreted as denoting the inferiority of the Negro group. A sense of inferiority affects the motivation of a child to learn. Segregation with the sanction of law, therefore, has a tendency to (retard) the educational and mental development of Negro children and to deprive them of some of the benefits they would receive in a racial(ly) integrated school system.

And the final conclusion was stated in these words:

We conclude that in the field of public education the doctrine of "separate but equal" has no place. Separate educational facilities are inherently unequal.

In view of these sweeping pronouncements, it is needless to extend the argument. There is nothing in the quoted statements of the court to suggest that the reasoning does not apply with equal force to colleges as to primary schools. Indeed it is fair to say that they apply with greater force to students of mature age in the concluding years of their formal education as they are about to engage in the serious business of adult life. . . .

Lesser v. Board of Education of The City of New York

Appellate Division of the New York Supreme Court
18 New York Appellate Division 2nd 388 (1963).

PER CURIAM:

The petitioner (the mother and guardian ad litem of Melvin Lesser, an infant) instituted this proceeding . . . to compel the Board of Education of the City of New York, the Board of Higher Education of the City of New York, the president of Brooklyn College, and the principal of Lafayette High School, to review the scholastic records of her son Melvin, to make corrections in his scholastic records and to admit him to Brooklyn College. The petitioner's prayer for relief has been granted; and the Boards of Education and the school officials appeal.

Melvin was graduated from Lafayette High School in 1962. During his attendance there, he was a member of the "Scholarship

Program" which consisted of a series of classes open to students of superior performance and in which a more enriched treatment of the subjects was offered, enabling the participating students to achieve the maximum of their capacity. His high school scholastic average was 84.3%. The petitioner complains that, despite her son's creditable accomplishments, he has been denied admission to Brooklyn College, a municipal college under the jurisdiction of the Board of Higher Education.

Brooklyn College has adopted standards governing the admission of students: (1) the completion of 16 units of high school subjects in prescribed courses; and (2) attainment of an average which is set for each term in order to accommodate the number of applicants as determined by budgetary allotments and college facilities. Like other institutions for higher education, Brooklyn College has received many more applications than may be accepted within the limits of its conveniences. Petitioner's son qualified under the first requirement, but his average of 84.3% was below the average of 85% set by the authorities for admission. Nor did he achieve the average required under an alternative method of admission used by the authorities—a method which was based on the mark achieved by the student on the college board aptitude test merged with the student's high school average.

The petitioner does not challenge the accuracy of the averages attributed to her son. She asserts instead that the admission officer should have given greater weight to the marks which her son had obtained in the subjects encompassed within the "Scholarship Program." Such an evaluation, she claims, would result in an average above the minimum 85%. Further, she attacks the fairness and validity of an admission policy which operates solely by means of mechanically-applied average. The court below sustained her contentions; it directed the appellants to redetermine Melvin's marks so as to bring them up to the 85% average, and then to admit him to the college.

In our opinion, the court was without power to make such directions. Courts may not interfere with the administrative discretion exercised by agencies which are vested with the administration and control of educational institutions, unless the circumstances disclosed by the record leave no scope for the use of that discretion in the manner under scrutiny. . . . If the Board of Higher Education performs its discretion fairly and not arbitrarily, the court may not substitute its judgment for that of the board. . . .

More particularly, a court should refrain from interjecting its views within those delicate areas of school administration which relate to the eligibility of applicants and the determination of marking standards, unless a clear abuse of statutory authority or a practice of discrimination or gross error has been shown. . . .

Petitioner's son was entitled to fair and equal treatment with other applicants in accordance with standards reasonably established. The record before us denotes no arbitrary, unfair, or unreasonable conduct by the appellants in denying him admission.

Whether, in computing the high school average, the marks given in special courses such as the "Scholarship Program" should be accorded more weight than the marks given in standard courses, was clearly a matter resting exclusively in the discretion of the school and college authorities. Equally, the determination as to what factors should enter into the standards set for college admission was within the exclusive province of the college authorities. The judicial task ends when it is found that the applicant has received from the college authorities uniform treatment under reasonable regulations fairly administered. In effect, by the order of the court below petitioner's son has been granted a preference over other applicants who may be equally worthy. This court may not do.

Williams v. McNair

United States District Court, D. South Carolina, 1970
316 F. Supp. 134.

DONALD RUSSELL, District Judge:

This is an action instituted by the plaintiffs, all males, suing on behalf of themselves and others similarly situated, to enjoin the enforcement of a State statute which limits regular admissions to Winthrop College, a state supported college located at Rock Hill, South Carolina, to "girls." They assert that, except for their sex, they fully meet the admission requirements of the college.

The defendants are the present members of the Board of Trustees of Winthrop College, as constituted under its enabling legislation.

It is clear from the stipulated facts that the State of South Carolina has established a wide range of educational institutions at the college and university level consisting of eight separate institutions, with nine additional regional campuses. The several institutions so established vary in purpose, curriculum, and location. Some are limited to undergraduate programs; others extend their offerings into the graduate field. With two exceptions, such institutions are co-educational. Two, by law, however, limit their student admissions to members of one sex. Thus the Citadel restricts its student admissions to males and Winthrop, the college involved in this proceeding, may not admit as a regular degree candidate males. There is an historical reason for these legislative restrictions upon the admission standard of these two latter institutions. Winthrop, . . . was designed as a school for young ladies, which, though offering a liberal arts program, gave special attention to many courses thought to be specifically helpful to female students.

The Equal Protection Clause of the Fourteenth Amendment does not require "identity of treatment" for all citizens, or preclude a state, by legislation, from making classifications and creating differences in the rights of different groups. It is only when the discriminatory treatment and varying standards, as created by the legislative or administrative classification are arbitrary and wanting in any rational justification that they offend the Equal Protection Clause. . . . Thus, the issue in this case is whether the discrimination in admission of students, created by the statute governing the operation of Winthrop and based on sex, is without rational justification. . . . It is no doubt true, as plaintiffs suggest, that the trend in this country is away from the operation of separate institutions for the sexes, but there is still a substantial number of private and public institutions, which limit their enrollment to one sex and do so because they feel it offers better educational advantages. While history and tradition alone may not support a discrimination, the Constitution does not require that a classification "keep abreast of the latest" in educational opinion, especially when there remains a respectable opinion to the contrary; it only demands that the discrimination not be wholly wanting in reason. Any other rule would mean that courts and not legislatures would determine all matters of public policy. It must be remembered, too, that Winthrop is merely a part of an entire system of State-supported higher education. It may not be considered in isolation. If the State operated only one college and that college was Winthrop, there can be no question that to deny males admission thereto would be impermissible under the Equal Protection Clause. But, as we have already remarked, these plaintiffs have a complete range of state institutions they may attend. They are free to attend either an all-male or, if they wish, a number of co-educational institutions at various locations over the State. There is no suggestion that there is any special feature connected with Winthrop that will make it more advantageous educationally to them than any number of other State-supported institutions. They point to no courses peculiar to Winthrop in which they wish to enroll. It is true that, in the case of some, if not all, of the plaintiffs, Winthrop is more convenient geographically for them than the other State institutions. They, in "being denied the right to attend the State college in their home town," are treated no differently than are other students who reside in communities many miles distant from any State supported college or university. The location of any such institution must necessarily inure to the benefit of some and to the detriment of others, depending upon the distance the affected individuals reside from the institution.

Under these circumstances, this Court cannot declare as a matter of law that a legislative classification, premised as it is on respectable pedagogical opinion, is without any rational justification and violative of the Equal Protection Clause. . . . Moreover, it may be, as plaintiffs argue, that the experience of the college in admitting in its summer and evening classes male students, has weakened to some extent the force of the legislative determination that the maintenance of at least one all-female institution in the state system has merit educationally. The evaluation of such experience, however, is not the function or prerogative of the Courts: that falls within the legislative province and the plaintiffs may address their arguments to that body and look to it for relief . . .

It is suggested by the plaintiffs that this conclusion is contrary to the ruling in *Kirstein v. Rector and Visitors of University of Virginia* (D.C. Va. 1970) 309 F. Supp. 184. The Court there very pointedly remarked, however, that "We are urged to go further and to hold that Virginia may not operate any educational institution separated according to the sexes. We decline to do so." Page 187, 309 F. Supp. There the women-plaintiffs were seeking admission to the University of Virginia and it was conceded that the University occupied a pre-eminence among the State-supported institutions of Virginia and offered a far wider range of curriculum. No such situation exists here. It is not intimated that Winthrop offers a wider range of subject matter or enjoys a position of outstanding prestige over the other State-supported institutions in this State whose admission policies are co-educational.

Let judgment be entered for the defendants.

2

TUITION AND FEES

Attendance at a college or university implies a student's acceptance of the obligation to pay tuition and fees, in addition to costs of a room, board, books, and numerous incidental expenses. The assumption of such obligations can create legal problems involving, for example, discrimination on the basis of residence when assessing tuition charges. Other problems include: What is the parents' responsibility for their child's educational expenses? Can a parent be forced to pay such costs? Can a minor student apply for financial aid without his parents' cooperation? What limitations can institutions of higher learning place on a student's conduct and studies in exchange for financial aid?

COSTS FOR NON-RESIDENTS

Although tuition is usually charged by both private and public universities and colleges, in the case of public institutions, state statutes or constitutions may preclude charging tuition to residents of the state or limit the amount that may be charged.[1] Such provisions often are silent regarding fees for out-of-state students, however. The power of university administrations to make regulations regarding residency requirements is unlimited at present, and legislative authority to distinguish between "in-state" and "out-of-state" students

[1] 15 *American Jurisprudence* 2d Colleges and Universities § 18 (1964).

is recognized by the courts.[2] University policies defining residency often use such criteria as voting status, payment of taxes, a waiting period, or, in the case of minor students, parents' residence. But current discontent with such requirements and an increasing willingness to challenge their constitutionality in the courts, in addition to the difficulty in applying the regulations, are leading to reevaluation if not abandonment of the rules.[3] Two legal problems arising involve equal protection under the Fourteenth Amendment of the United States Constitution and the problem of establishing residency by the non-resident minor.[4]

Regulations requiring a six- to twelve-month waiting period prior to initial enrollment at a state university for the purpose of establishing residency are supported on the theory that such regulations prevent a heavy influx of students into the state to take advantage of educational benefits.[5] These regulations, which may also provide that the student's non-resident status will remain unchanged throughout his attendance at the university, are being attacked under the theory that classifying citizens by the length of time they have lived in a state is unreasonable and arbitrary[6] in that it is an unconstitutional interference with the right of interstate travel.[7] Such a right was recognized by the Supreme Court in *Shapiro v. Thompson,*[8] in which it struck down the one-year waiting period provided for in state welfare laws. But the California Court of Appeal in *Kirk* refused to make an analogy between state expenditures for welfare and state expenditures for education, holding that attendance at a public institution of higher education does not present ". . . an immediate and pressing need for preservation of life and health of persons unable to live without public assistance."[9] It should be noted however, that in the *Kirk* case the court was dealing with a provision

---

[2]*Landwehr v. Regents of the University of Colorado,* 156 Colo. 1 (1964).
[3]38 *University of Missouri, Kansas City Law Review* 341, 354 (1970).
[4]*Ibid.,* at 342.
[5]*Ibid.,* at 344-345.
[6]*Ibid.,* at 343.
[7]*Kirk v. Board of Regents of the University of California,* 78 Cal. Rptr. 260 (1969).
[8]394 U.S. 618 (1969).
[9]78 Cal. Rptr. 260. Also see *Starns v. Malkerson,* 326 F. Supp. 234 (1970), affirmed 91 S. Ct. 1231 (Mar. 29, 1971).

that permitted the student to establish in-state status after one year's residence.

The constitutionality of waiting periods (up to one year) for establishing residency for tuition purposes has been upheld so far. But courts have refused to accept a provision that would force retention of out-of-state status throughout a student's attendance at a university. In the Iowa case *Clarke v. Redeker*,[10] a university regulation stated that students from other states who were enrolled in any state educational institution would be presumed to be in Iowa primarily for educational purposes, and would be considered not to have established residence in Iowa.[11] Although the court did not object to the regulation, it ruled that twenty-two-year-old Clarke, although a resident of Illinois at the time of his initial enrollment, had overcome the state's presumption that he had come to Iowa for educational purposes only by his marriage to a resident of Iowa and by his expression of intention to practice law in that state after graduation from the College of Law.

Clarke is an example of the trend toward allowing emancipated[12] minors, as well as students who have reached their majority,[13] if they are emancipated, to establish residency after a waiting period requirement has been fulfilled, even though they were not residents at time of initial enrollment. But conversely, emancipation or reaching majority does not automatically establish residency if the waiting period requirement has *not* been fulfilled. This has been shown by the California Court of Appeal's refusal to accept the common law rule that a woman automatically becomes a resident of her husband's state by marriage—at least not for purposes of tuition reduction.[14]

University regulations defining a student's residency status at the time of initial enrollment are often used to force him to keep

[10]259 F. Supp. 117 (Iowa, 1966).

[11]*Ibid.*, at 122.

[12]"Emancipation may occur by virtue of the child's marriage, his entrance into the armed forces, his getting a job and becoming self-supporting, and in other ways." H. Clark, Domestic Relations 505 (1st ed. 1968).

[13]"An infant reaches majority at the age of twenty-one years, unless a different period is prescribed by state statute." 43 *Corpus Juris Secundum* Infants § 2 (1945). Ratification of the Twenty-sixth Amendment to the Constitution is likely to have an impact here.

[14]78 Cal. Rptr. 260.

non-resident status once he has reached majority if he is not emancipated (he still receives parental financial aid). As long as emancipation is the key to residency, the student receiving parental aid is
classified according to his parents' place of residence. It is argued,
however, "The fact that the student does not support himself is not
an accurate index of ability to determine residence. A student should
not be forced to choose between giving up his source of support
while attending the university and having to pay non-resident tuition."[15] The argument continues:

If a student is old enough to marry, get a job, join the armed forces, and
become self-supporting, but chooses instead to exercise his right to go on to
the university to further his education, the law and the university should
not punish the [student] by forcing him to pay more money because he
cannot legally change his residence.[16]

An Arizona case[17] may prove to have significant bearing upon
future decisions involving non-resident student status. The facts of
the case reveal that the Regents of the University of Arizona adopted
a "One Year Residency" Rule for out-of-state students. Failure to
satisfy the Rule required the payment of fees not assessed the resident attending the university.

In its opinion, the court held that "Residence" is a state of mind
existent in the individual, accompanied by a physical presence within
the state. The state of mind can be manifested in many ways. There
is no set activity or activities that can provide a set proclamation
of intent. Each case must be considered separately. The court did
set forth some indicia of intent, however. They are: (1) register to
vote, (2) buy property, (3) acquire a driver's license, (4) purchase a
car and obtain local title, (5) work, (6) open a bank account, or
(7) marry.

The court among its findings held that the "One Year Residency" Rule represented an infringement on the freedom of interstate
movement under the Commerce Clause of the United States Constitution and was in violation of the Equal Protection Clause of the

[15]38 *University of Missouri, Kansas City Law Review* 341, 351-352.

[16]*Ibid.*, at 351.

[17]*Harper, et al. v. Arizona Board of Regents*, Superior Court of the State of Arizona,
County of Pima, No. 111657, 1970. Also see *Kirk v. Douglas*, 489 P.2d 201 (1971), and
Seran v. Douglas, 489 P.2d 601 (1971), where marriage changed the non-resident sta-
tus of the students.

Fourteenth Amendment. The decision was careful not to suggest that one could achieve resident status merely by attending the university. Clearly it takes intent and physical presence. On the other hand, attendance at the university should not preclude a person from attaining residency within Arizona.

Harper acknowledges the fluidity of population movement in the United States today. It assesses realistically the peripatetic nature of our college students made possible by modern modes of transportation. The ruling in the case departs from the reasoning usually applied to questions on non-resident status. It may represent an important development in this area.

COSTS FOR ALL STUDENTS

Although non-resident tuition cases are more numerous, there are several significant decisions bearing on tuition charges for state residents. As a general rule, tuition fees for "in-state" students are valid unless statutes or the constitution prohibit tuition or limit its amount.[18] Distinctions are often made between costs of actual instruction and costs of other pupil services, such as athletic facilities, student unions, laboratory fees, health care, and building maintenance.[19] Statutory prohibitions against exacting tuition fees often do not include these incidental expenses, and courts have upheld both legislatures' right to assess such fees and universities' right to collect them.[20]

In the case of private institutions, the right to charge tuition is based on contract theory, and such fees may be charged even when the private university is chartered by a "free-tuition" state. In fact, the contract theory applies to all fees legally assessed by both public and private institutions, and governs refund as well as payment of such fees.

A student who withdraws before the end of a semester is not always entitled to refund of all money paid, for institutions have a right to collect a proportionate part of the costs for ". . . board, tuition, supplies and incidentals . . ." for the period of actual

[18]15 *American Jurisprudence* 2d Colleges and Universities § 18 (1964).

[19]*State ex rel Priest v. Regents of the University of Wisconsin,* 54 Wisc. 159 (1882). See also *State v. Regents of the University System of Georgia,* 179 Ga. 210 (1934).

[20]*State ex rel. Veeder v. State Board of Education,* 97 Mont. 121 (1934).

attendance.[21] Some courts will allow a university to collect fees assessed after a student has withdrawn.[22] But university regulations stating that in those cases of withdrawal "without cause, suspension, or expulsion" the student must absorb the loss for the entire semester, payment will not be enforced in the absence of proof that the student was within those categories.[23] Nor will such regulations be enforced by the courts when it is found that a university did not sufficiently inform a student regarding the regulation, even though it was printed in the school's bulletin.[24] A physical disability that prevents a student from pursuing productively his academic program may entitle him to a refund or relieve him of the obligation to pay the balance of tuition, even in the face of catalogue statements that such fees are non-refundable.[25]

Campus turmoil requiring the cancellation of classes has raised an interesting question bearing upon tuition. In a New York case,[26] a father of a student at N.Y.U. sought a refund of tuition for nineteen days of classes when instruction was suspended in May 1970, during student disorders over the invasion of Cambodia. The action was brought in the Small Claims Court of New York City, and alleged that the defendant-university breached its contract by cancelling classes. The Court found a breach of contract and ruled in favor of the plaintiff, awarding him a $277.40 refund.

On appeal the case was reversed.[27] The Appellate Court reasoned that N.Y.U., a private institution, is governed by academic self-regulation, and where there is no arbitrary and capricious action there is no reason for the courts to interfere. The Court observed:

. . . In the light of the events on the defendant's campus and in college communities throughout the country on May 4th to 5th, 1970, the Court [Small Claims] erred in substituting its judgment for that of the University administrators and in concluding that the University was unjustified in

[21]*Aynesworth v. Peacock Military College*, 225 S.W. 866 (1920) Texas.

[22]*Pierce v. Peacock Military College*, 220 S.W. 191 (1920) Texas.

[23]*Rogers v. Councill*, 266 S.W. 207 (1924) Texas.

[24]*Drucker v. New York University*, 57 Misc. 2d 937 (1968) New York, reversed on other grounds in *Drucker v. New York University*, 59 Misc. 2d 789 (1969).

[25]*Holton v. Cook*, 181 Ark. 806 (1930).

[26]*Paynter v. New York University*, 314 N.Y.S.2d 676 (1970).

[27]*Paynter v. New York University*, 319 N.Y.S.2d 893 (1971).

suspending classes for the time remaining in the school year prior to the examination period. Moreover, while in a strict sense, a student contracts with a college or university for a number of courses to be given during the academic year, the services rendered by the university cannot be measured by the time spent in the classroom. The circumstances of the relationship permit the implication that the professor or the colleges may make minor changes in this regard. The insubstantial change made in the schedule of classes does not permit a recovery of tuition.

The traditional approach of the courts in college and university cases is visible here. Unless there is clear abuse of the self-regulation principle, the courts will not intervene. The abuse, remember, must be substantial.

PARENTAL RESPONSIBILITY FOR COSTS

It is interesting to observe that the father of the student brought the action in the N.Y.U. case. When tuition and fees are discussed, inevitably the question is raised, who actually is responsible for paying college costs if a student is an unemancipated minor? There remains some confusion on this point, but a decided trend favors recognition of the principle that the father is responsible.[28] There are decisions holding that a parent cannot be required to defray college costs, however.[29]

In those cases following the majority rule of parental obligation to support the student, the courts acknowledge that a college education is now a necessity of life.[30]

. . . The fact is that the importance of a college education is being more and more recognized in matters of commerce, society, government, and all human relations, and the college graduate is being more and more preferred over those who are not so fortunate. No parent should subject his worthy child to this disadvantage if he has the financial capacity to avoid it.

The requirement of course presumes the parent's ability to pay and the child's ability to learn. The courts will consider these factors

[28]36 *New York University Law Review* 634-635 (1961).

[29]*Haag v. Haag*, 240 Ind. 291 (1959).

[30]*Pass v. Pass*, 238 Miss. 449 (1960).

in deciding these cases. Each will be decided on its own merits and, depending on the financial assets available, child support can range from bare subsistence up to and including private school tuition.

As a general rule, one's father, unless he is dead or is unable to do so because of disability or other reasonable cause, has the main responsibility to support his children. Usually the matter of support does not become an issue unless the parents seek a divorce. Whether an unemancipated child could sue his or her father for college support in a proceeding not involving a divorce settlement remains to be answered. Some states prohibit suits against parents by their unemancipated minors except in divorce suits.

It is known, however, that there are limits on the support a parent must provide for his offspring. Decisions in the New York Family Court[31] and the subsequent appeal of the case[32] are revealing. In a "John Doe" and "Mary Roe" proceeding (to assure the anonymity of the parties), the Family Court held that "even though a young women had not met all her father's conditions for support, he must continue to pay his twenty-year-old daughter's college tuition and living expenses until she reached the age of twenty-one." The decision went on to hold that a parent ". . . does not have the right to impose unreasonable conditions that are not in the best interests of the child." In this case, the father objected to the life style adopted by his daughter while attending a metropolitan institution of higher education.

Later, in a four to one decision by the Appellate Division of the New York State Supreme Court, the decision holding the father responsible was reversed. In rejecting the earlier ruling, the Appeals Court stated: "The father—in return for his maintenance and support—is entitled to set reasonable standards, rules and regulations for his child."

The opinion emphasized that the daughter had deceived the father by living off campus when he wanted her to live in a dormitory. It was further found that she was experimenting with drugs and refused to return home at her father's request. The decision did not find the father's actions to be capricious and went on to say: "If the daughter chose not to comply, at her age, that may be her

[31]Orders entered on August 21, 1970, and November 30, 1970.
[32]*Roe v. Doe,* 36 A.D.2d 162, New York (1971).

prerogative; but she cannot have her cake and eat it too. The father not only has the right, but the obvious duty to guide and direct the child."

Parental financial assistance is the major source of support for students attending college. Only a small percentage of students defray the total costs of their education. Even in cases when the student turns to the institution or government for financial aid, parental cooperation is necessary to obtain the scholarship, grant, or loan. Since most awards are made according to financial need, many private and public institutions rely on an accurate assessment of parents' income and ability to contribute. Unless one can secure parental cooperation to supply the necessary information, a student may be denied consideration. This policy appears to prejudice the student unfairly. It would make an interesting issue for judicial consideration.

The financial aid situation is further complicated by the law in some states that persons under a specified age cannot be held responsible for their own debts. Parents are required to co-sign educational loans. One solution proposed is the *Uniform Minor Student Capacity to Borrow Act*,[33] which would do away with the requirement of co-signers for loans from universities, banks, or trust companies. The proposal, modifications of which have been enacted in New York and North Carolina,[34] reads:

Any written obligation signed by a minor sixteen or more years of age in consideration of an educational loan received by him from any person is enforceable as if he were an adult at the time of execution, but only if prior to the making of the educational loan an educational institution has certified that the minor is enrolled, or has been accepted for enrollment in the educational institution.[35]

The newly created deferred tuition plan must meet this question of the incapacity of minors to enter into a legal and binding contract.

[33]Proposed in 1969 by the National Conference of Commissioners of Uniform State Laws and The American Bar Association.

[34]N.Y. Education Law § 281 (McKinney 1969); North Carolina Gen. Stat. 116-174.1 (Michie 1966).

[35]T. E. Blackwell, *College Law Manual*, 1970 Supp., Santa Monica, Cal., pp. 4-5.

Under the plan, students would pay off college tuition costs from post-graduation earnings over a 20- to 30-year period. There is every reason to believe that the *Uniform Minor Student Capacity to Borrow Act* or a comparable provision would be found acceptable in the various states to implement a plan of deferred tuition and/or to provide other means for college students to obtain financial aid free of parental involvement.

SPECIAL-PURPOSE FINANCIAL AID

Until proposals as outlined above are enacted by states or the legal age limit is reduced by legislative act, however, students remain dependent on state and federal governments and private sources for educational funds. What then in the way of restrictions may legally be placed on the conduct and studies of students who receive such aid?

States often provide scholarship funds for students with specific career interests. For example, the State of Connecticut provides more than one hundred scholarships for students attending the state colleges, to be awarded on the basis of scholarship, general fitness, and need, but with preference given to those who intend to teach in the public schools of the state.[36] Vermont legislation encourages the study of medicine.[37] Generally, if a scholarship recipient does not fulfill his commitment to undertake a career as specified in the legislation, he incurs the obligation to repay the money as a loan. The justification for "special treatment" of these students is that, in the eyes of the state, it has an interest in promoting the educational careers of those who in the future will contribute to the state. The federal government also encourages students to enter specific fields by awarding scholarships and grants.[38]

But what is the status of restricted scholarships, intended for persons belonging to specified groups only: Can a state, or its agent, restrict the use of scholarship funds on the basis of race, religion, or geography? Can a private institution do the same? Can the federal

[36]Conn. Gen. Stat. § 10-112 (Rev. 1958, Supp. 1971).

[37]16 V.S.A. 2362 (Equity 1968).

[38]United States Military Academy, 10 U.S.C. 4342 (1965); grants for teaching in the education of handicapped children, 20 U.S.C. 611 (1965); and Assistance to Nursing Students, 42 U.S.C. 297 (1965).

government restrict the use of its funds to only those students who avoid involvement in campus disruptions?

A state may legally classify persons for purposes of scholarship aid if such classification is reasonable in terms of a legitimate state objective, such as increasing the state's supply of teachers or doctors. Decisions of the Supreme Court since the early 1950's on racial restrictions make it extremely doubtful that the exclusion of minority groups from consideration for financial aid is reasonable in the field of education.[39] But what of scholarships established solely for the benefit of a minority group—can the constitutionality of these admittedly restrictive grants be upheld? One justification offered holds that:

The equal protection mandate requires the state either to treat all its people alike, or, if it gives special treatment to some, to have a good reason for doing so. . . . As long as the state educational policy in practice provides all its citizens and residents with the same opportunity to attend college on an equal basis, there might be no objection to instances of special help to minorities which by common knowledge are known to need such additional aid. . . . The same should apply to any other minority group whose need for such extra help is demonstrable or commonly recognized.[40]

Yet this reasoning does not do away with the problem that the student is singled out for inclusion in or exclusion from a scholarship program because of his race. A better solution might be to make scholarship funds available to qualified individuals on the basis of need and merit alone.

In the case of state supported institutions administering scholarship funds that are provided by private donors and are restricted to members of a particular faith:

. . . such preferential treatment accorded to members of the specified religions, when performed by a state agency, appears to be contrary to the Fourteenth Amendment, since a classification on the basis of religion seems to have no reasonable relationship to the objectives of state education. In addition . . . there is serious doubt that the First Amendment permits a state agency to dispense scholarship funds within its control on the basis of religious affiliation, even where the funds are from private sources.[41]

[39]33 New York University Law Review 604, 606 (1958).
[40]Ibid., at 607-608.
[41]Ibid., at 609.

Geographically-restricted scholarships confine grants to residents of a particular state, county, school district, or city. The argument in favor of such restrictions—that since residents largely provide such funds, residents should also benefit to a greater degree than do non-residents—ignores the resulting inequality of opportunity between wealthy areas and poorer areas. But the constitutional right of states to discriminate in favor of their own citizens is well established. The Equal Protection Clause prevents discrimination among residents of the state, but it does not prevent preferential treatment of all residents over non-residents.[42]

In summary, under the Equal Protection Clause of the Fourteenth Amendment, a state institution cannot administer a scholarship program that is racially discriminatory, restricted as to religion, or restricted (among its residents) on an unreasonable geographical basis, whether the funds come from public or private sources.[43]

A private college does not come within the scope of the Fourteenth Amendment, however, unless the state is sufficiently involved in its affairs that the school can be said to have lost its private character. In the absence of substantial state involvement (the boundaries of which have yet to be defined by the courts), a private school is still free to discriminate in its admission and scholarship policies on any basis it chooses, unless it is prohibited from doing so by a state statute.[44]

RESTRICTIONS ON FINANCIAL AID FOR CAMPUS DISORDER

Although discrimination on the basis of race, religion, or geography is prohibited, a prohibition of another kind appears to be acknowledged by both state and federal government. This is legislation to combat campus disorders. By late 1970, 31 states had ennacted campus anti-riot laws.[45] A typical law is the Maryland provision:

[42]*Ibid.*, at 610.
[43]*Ibid.*, at 614.
[44]*Ibid.*, at 615. Also see *Ryan v. Hofstra University*, 324 N.Y.S. 2d 964 (1971).
[45]*Chronicle of Higher Education*, November 26, 1970, p. 6.

[It] prohibits disturbance of the orderly conduct of any school, college, or university, and the molesting or threatening of any one lawfully on or in the vicinity of a school. Violation is a misdemeanor subject to fine up to $1,000 or imprisonment for six months, or both.[46]

The Congress of the United States has also acted on this matter. Congress implements such sanctions by attaching riders to appropriations and authorization bills, providing that no part of the funds appropriated under the Acts shall go to such individuals.[47] These provisions raise several constitutional issues, and although ". . . it appears that no school has refused to implement a federal rider, a number of schools have refused to enforce various state-aid withdrawal riders."[48]

Responsibility for administration of the federal riders is delegated by the government agencies to the colleges and universities, who are provided with few guidelines indicating what severity of conduct justifies withdrawal of an individual's aid. Six of the ten unrest riders, in whole or in part, require criminal conviction as a prerequisite to withdrawal of aid.[49] Nor has every such bill adopted the model rider's provision that ". . . such limitation upon the use of money appropriated in this Act shall not apply to a particular individual until the appropriate institution of higher education . . . shall have had the opportunity to initiate or has completed such

[46]Article 27, 123 A of the Annotated Code Laws 1970, Ch 726, effective July 1, 1970.

[47]Public Law 92-48, Section 305 for the use of the U.S. Office of Education and Related Agencies Appropriation Act of 1972 provides: "No part of the funds appropriated under this Act shall be used to provide a loan, guarantee of a loan, a grant, the salary of or any remuneration whatever to any individual applying for admission, attending, employed by, teaching at, or doing research at an institution of higher education who has engaged in conduct on or after August 1, 1969, which involves the use of (or the assistance to others in the use of) force or the threat of force or the seizure of property under the control of an institution of higher education, to require or prevent the availability of certain curriculum, or to prevent the faculty, administrative officials, or students in such institution from engaging in their duties or pursuing their studies at such an institution."

[48]*The Corporation of Haverford College et al. v. Reecher et al.*, 329 F. Supp. 1196 (1971). Also see *Undergraduate Student Association of the University of Illinois at Champaign v. Peltason*, Civ. Action No.___ (N.D. Ill., filed December 1971).

[49]22 *Stanford Law Review* 1094, 1103 (1970).

proceedings as it deems appropriate . . . to determine whether the provisions of this limitation upon the use of appropriated funds shall apply."[50] But the issue of whether the schools have the discretion not to put the aid-withdrawal machinery into effect has not been resolved. Indeed, educational institutions have seldom employed the unrest riders in dealing with student disorders. Although more than 9,000 separate protest incidents occurred on two-thirds of the nation's college campuses during the 1969-70 academic year, a total of only 440 students lost federal aid during fiscal year 1971 as a result of their participation in campus riots and disruptions. Similarly, a mere 86 out of a national total of approximately 2,600 colleges withheld funds from students or faculty because of participation in disruptive activities.[51]

CONCLUSION

Although tuition and fees seldom pay more than one-third of the cost of a college education, the expense of attending institutions of higher education is reaching alarming proportions. Amounts of $4,000 and $5,000 are not unheard of for private schools. Public colleges supported by tax funds may no longer provide education without assessing the student substantial charges. Even with public support, state college and university students are faced with minimum annual expenses of $1,500 to $2,000. As a result, the subject of college tuition and fees is not an inconsequential matter, and questions involving this subject are often brought before the courts for litigation. In dealing with this topic, the distinction between public and private institutions must immediately be drawn. In the former instance, students attending public colleges may not be required to pay tuition and fees. Unless there is a legislative prohibition, however, tuition and fees may be collected. On the other hand, tuition in private schools is based on a contract theory between the institution and the student. All the principles of contract law apply in such a relationship.

Public colleges and universities provide free tuition or reduced

[50]*Ibid.*, n. 23.
[51]*Today's Education*, Vol. 59, No. 9, December 1970.

tuition for the benefit of their residents, and thereby non-residents of the state do not qualify for this preferred treatment. Yet a non-resident can obtain residency by meeting certain criteria. Once these standards are met and residency attaches, the individual is treated as any other citizen of the state for the purpose of tuition charges.

The ratification of the 26th Amendment in 1971, which gives 18-year-olds the right to vote in all elections, has interjected a new issue in the non-resident tuition debate. A majority of the states have recognized the right of students to vote in their college towns.[52] Once a voting residence has been established, can the student be considered a non-resident? A State District Court in Kansas has ruled that a student who registers to vote in a college town no longer is subject to non-residency fees.[53] Further decisions are anticipated in this area that will provide a more definitive picture of what rules should be applied to this area.

Parents, more specifically the father, are responsible for providing financial support to defray the college costs of their children. Although some courts do not recognize this general rule, it is widely accepted unless the father is financially unable to bear the cost. A New York case, however, does not hold the father responsible if the child defies his reasonable request for proper behavior.

The states and the federal government provide scholarship and loan support to encourage students to enter specific career fields. No government, municipal, state, or federal, can administer financial aid programs contrary to the principles of the U.S. Constitution. Racial discrimination, religious restrictions, and other unreasonable discriminatory practices are forbidden. But funds for scholarships and loans can be prohibited or terminated by legislation ennacted to curb campus disturbances.

---

[52]*Chronicle of Higher Education*, April 3, 1972, p. 1 and 3. Also see *Jolicoeur v. Mihaly*, 96 Cal. Rptr. 697 (1971) and *Wilkins v. Bentley*, 189 N.W.2d 423 (1971).

[53]*Higher Education and National Affairs*, January 14, 1972, p. 5.

Stringer v. Gould

Supreme Court of New York, 1970

64 Misc. 2d 89

HAROLD E. KOREMAN, Justice:

The petition seeks an order in this proceeding directing the Board of Trustees of the University of the State of New York to rescind its resolution of May 9, 1968, as it relates to a mandatory student activity fee, or, in the alternative, to prescribe guidelines regulating the disbursement of the funds created by the activity fees by prohibiting their use for certain alleged unauthorized purposes. It is also sought to prevent disbursement of funds alleged to have been unlawfully appropriated for political and other purposes, to which members of the student body opposed to such programs and activities are compelled to give financial support, and to prevent appropriations and expenditures of any additional funds for such purposes. The resolution in question authorized the student body at each State-operated campus to fix and assess upon themselves, either directly or through duly elected representatives on the student council or other organization chosen by the student body, an annual fee for the support of programs of an educational, cultural, recreational and social nature approved by the student organization elected by and representative of the student body. The resolution also provides that every student is required to pay the activities fee upon registration, and, in any case where a student has been allowed to register without payment of the fee, the administrative officers of the particular State University campus concerned may withhold grades or transcripts of credits until such obligation has been met. Prior to the adoption of this resolution the State University operated under a student activity fee imposed and administered by the students, payment of which was purely voluntary on the part of any student. It is not disputed that the State University authorities adopted the resolution of May 9, 1968, in an attempt to make payment of the activity fee a requirement before a student could register at the University, and to change a voluntary fee, which was found to be unsatisfactory, to a mandatory fee.

The fundamental issue before the court is whether the Trustees of the University also divested themselves of any further duties or responsibilities relating to the use or administration of the activities fund by adopting this resolution. If the Trustees still retain control of the fund it becomes subject to the requirements of law for disbursement of State funds since payment of the fee has been made mandatory. The Attorney General contends on behalf of the respondents who are the officials of the State University that they have authorized the student body to impose the fee and have no voice or control over any appropriations or expenditures of the fund. However, the Attorney General concedes that sanctions may be imposed for failure to pay the fee, and that any appropriations made by the students for the activities fund must be limited to educational, cultural, recreational or social purposes.

In view of the requirement for payment of the activities fee before a student may be registered, and the fact that grades and transcripts may be withheld for failure to pay, the trustees have efficiently established a mandatory activities fee. In the court's opinion it cannot be said that the officials of the University have no voice over appropriations or expenditures of the fund since appropriations may be made by the students only for the purposes permitted by the trustees. . . .

It is not the fuction of this court to pass upon the propriety of any of the programs or activities proposed or approved by the Central Council of the Student Association. Nor is it within the province of the courts to determine in each instance whether a student sponsored program or activity is educational, cultural, recreational or social in nature. Interference in matters involving the internal affairs, administration and supervision of the State University would have the anomalous result of usurpation by the courts of the powers and duties vested in the trustees by the legislature. Since the responsibility of administration and supervision in this area rests with the trustees, appropriations or expenditures of the fund in question may not be made without the approval of the trustees as to the purposes for such appropriations and expenditures.

Accordingly, the Central Council of the Student Association is prohibited and enjoined from expending any monies of the fund already appropriated for student extracurricular activities, and from making any further appropriations of the fund for such activities without first obtaining the determination and approval of the trustees as to whether they are educational, cultural, recreational or social in nature.

Starns et al. v. A. Malkerson et al.
United States District Court, D. Minnesota
326 F. Supp. 234

MILES W. LORD, District Judge:

The Board of Regents of the University of Minnesota has promulgated a regulation which provides in part that, "No student is eligible for residence classification in the University . . . unless he has been a bona fide domiciliary of the state for at least a year immediately prior thereto." The effect of this regulation is to impose on any person moving into the state a one year durational residency requirement to qualify as a resident for tuition purposes at the University. This case raises the issue of whether the regulation is unconstitutional as violative of the Equal Protection Clause. For reasons which follow, we have concluded in the negative.

The plaintiffs married their husbands in 1968 while their husbands were enrolled in the School of Law of the University of Chicago. In June of 1969, plaintiffs moved to Minnesota with their husbands who had obtained employment in Minnesota. Neither plaintiffs nor their husbands claim residency in Minnesota for purposes of this action prior to June 1969. Both plaintiffs enrolled as full-time students at the University for the 1969-1970 school year and were classified as nonresident students by the University. This meant they were required to pay tuition in an amount more than double that they would have had to pay had they been classified as resident students. The classification of the plaintiffs as nonresident students was made pursuant to the Board of Regents' tuition regulations. . . .

At the outset it is important to note what is *not* at issue in this case. Plaintiffs do not challenge the right of the University to charge nonresident students higher tuition than that paid by residents. . . . Nor do the plaintiffs challenge the right of the University to use a durational residency test as a rebuttable presumption of nonresidency. . . . The sole issue here is whether it is constitutionally permissible for a state to create an irrebuttable presumption that any person who has not continuously resided in Minnesota for one year immediately before his entrance to the University is a nonresident for tuition purposes. . . .

Plaintiffs assert that we are dealing here with the infringement of a basic, fundamental right—the right to interstate movement—and thus we must apply the "compelling state interest" test. Plaintiffs rely on *Shapiro v. Thompson*, 394 U.S. 618, in which the Supreme Court declared unconstitutional state and the District of Columbia statutory provisions denying welfare assistance to residents who had not resided within their jurisdictions for at least one year immediately preceding their application for such assistance. In that case the Court held that the one-year waiting period for welfare assistance served to penalize the exercise of the constitutional right to travel and thus, unless the classification was shown to be necessary to promote a compelling governmental interest, it was unconstitutional. The plaintiffs argue here that, "The inescapable effect of the one-year residence requirement is to deter persons from moving into the state in order to establish a new residence . . . or, when the deterence was insufficient, to disadvantage them on account of their exercise of liberty of movement." Thus, they claim that the classification created by the regulation must also be shown to be necessary to promote a compelling governmental interest to be constitutionally permissible.

We believe that this case is distinguishable from *Shapiro* in two important respects. First, in *Shapiro* the Supreme Court found, based on weighty evidence, that the one-year waiting period for welfare assistance had as a specific objective the exclusion from the jurisdiction of the poor who needed or may need relief. The Court stated that such a purpose could not serve as a "justification for the classification created by the one-year waiting period, since that purpose is constitutionally impermissible."

Here, by contrast, there are no state of facts upon which this Court could posit, as a finding of fact, that the one-year waiting period for resident tuition purposes has as a specific objective excluding or even deterring out-of-state students from attending the

University. The record indicates, in fact, that of the approximately 50,000 students enrolled in the University in the fall of 1968, over 6,000 were nonresidents. In view of these statistics, we believe that the one-year waiting period does not deter any appreciable number of persons from moving into the state. There is no basis in the record to conclude, therefore, that the operation of the one-year waiting period has an unconstitutional "chilling effect" on the assertion of the constitutional right to travel.

Second, in *Shapiro* the one-year waiting period for welfare assistance had the effect of denying the basic necessities of life to needy residents. Thus, the deterring effect on interstate movement by the use of the residency requirement was readily apparent. . . .

There is no showing here that the one-year waiting period has any dire effects on the nonresident student equivalent to those noted in *Shapiro*. There is less likelihood, therefore, that the one-year waiting period to acquire resident status for tuition purposes would make a person hesitate when deciding to establish residency in Minnesota and to apply to the University. . . .

For the above reasons, we conclude that this is not a case of an infringement of a fundamental right and thus the exacting standards of the compelling state interest test have no application. Unlike *Shapiro*, we find the one-year durational residence requirement challenged here does not constitute a penalty upon the exercise of the constitutional right of interstate travel and thus the regulation's constitutionality should be tested under the traditional equal protection standards. . . .

Plaintiffs assert that the one-year waiting period to acquire resident status for tuition purposes, since it is set up in terms of an absolute classification which is irrebuttable, is arbitrary and unreasonable. . . .

We believe it is reasonable to presume that a person who has not resided within the State for a year is a nonresident student, and that it is reasonable to require that to rebut this presumption the student must be a bona fide domiciliary of the State for one year. . . .

We turn, then, to the final question of whether the classification of the plaintiffs as nonresident students for tuition purposes is reasonably related to a legitimate objective of the State of Minnesota.

Plaintiffs contend that the one-year waiting period serves no

valid state purpose. They claim that viewing the possible justifica-
tions for the durational requirement, the regulation's only possible
purpose and effect is to deter students or potential students from becoming residents of the State and to punish them severely if they
become residents of the State. Defendants advance several grounds
which they argue are valid State objectives served by the one-year
waiting period. We need not, of course, explore all the grounds the
defendants advance in justification of the regulation. It is enough
that a solid foundation for the regulation can be found in any one of
the grounds set forth.

The primary justification the defendants assert is that the one-
year waiting period to acquire resident status for tuition purposes
is a rational attempt by the State to achieve partial cost equaliza-
tion between those who have and those who have not recently contributed to the State's economy through employment, tax payments
and expenditures therein. . . .

We believe that once the law affords recognition to the right of
a State to discriminate in tuition charges between a resident and
nonresident, that right to discriminate may be applied reasonably to
the end that a person retains a nonresident classification for tuition
purposes until he has completed a twelve-month period of domicile
within the State. We believe that the State of Minnesota has the right
to say that those new residents of the State shall make some contribution, tangible or intangible, towards the State's welfare for a period
of twelve months before becoming entitled to enjoy the same privileges as long-term residents possess to attend the University at a
reduced resident's fee. Accordingly, we hold that the regulation
requiring a one-year domicile within the State to acquire resident
classification for tuition purposes at the University is constitutionally
valid.

3

GRADES, CREDITS, AND GRADUATION

In this chapter we consider cases decided by the courts concerning the rights of students to question the evaluation made of their academic performance. Most of the cases arose when a student sought judicial review of his dismissal from a professional school. Perhaps this is a result of the fact that professional schools enroll relatively older and more sophisticated students with greater awareness of the legal remedies available, or that such institutions possess a great sense of responsibility to a profession and are particularly stringent in passing on the qualifications of their graduates. Undergraduates may decide it is too expensive in time and money to challenge individual decisions.

Colleges and universities have broad discretion in matters relating to dismissals and withholding of degrees and diplomas. Coupled with this is the traditional reticence of courts to involve themselves in the internal matters of institutions of higher learning. Unless a plaintiff can prove serious abuse of discretion on the part of college officials, the law courts will not interfere. This policy of noninterference is followed not only in the law's dealings with matters pertaining to education, but in other fields. Through the experience of centuries of Anglo-American jurisprudence, the courts have refrained from imposing their judgment in areas beyond their competence unless justice clearly requires intervention. Intervention is then limited to righting the wrong and not to second-guessing the decisions of the professional fields' experts.

For example, if the faculty of an institution has the power to pass upon the qualifications of a prospective graduate and it decides to withhold the degree, the courts will not review the faculty's decision. In *People ex rel. Jones v. New York Homeopathic Medical College and Hospital*,[1] the Superior Court of New York City ruled that it would not question the basis for the faculty's denial of the degree to a student, even though he alleged that the faculty had acted in bad faith. Since the courts ". . . must be careful not to infringe upon the discretion vested in . . . colleges," the court refused to grant relief. It observed, "The court cannot re-examine the plaintiff as to his qualifications to practice medicine, nor go over the studies in which he is said to be deficient."[2]

A case in which a student-plaintiff might have had a cause of action against the faculty, if he could have proved malice on its part, was *Steinhauer v. Arkins*.[3] The faculty of the Colorado State School of Mines refused to grant a degree to Steinhauer. He appealed to the school's Board of Trustees, but since the power to grant degrees rested in the faculty alone, the Board was bound by the faculty's judgment regarding a student's qualifications. Steinhauer brought suit against the Board, but the Court of Appeals dismissed the complaint, holding that the Board was not the proper party to be sued. The responsibility for deciding qualifications for graduation rested with the faculty, not the Trustees, and therefore no action was possible against the latter. If judicial relief was to be forthcoming, Steinhauer would have had to initiate a suit against the faculty.

Having decided that the proper parties are before it, a court may agree to examine the facts of a case. If such facts justify the discretion exercised by college administrators, review will be denied.

---

[1] 20 N.Y.S. 379 (1892). Similar rulings are found in *Tate v. North Pacific College*, 70 Or. 160 (1914), and *People ex rel. Pacella v. Bennett Medical College*, 205 Ill. App. 324 (1917).

[2] *Ibid.*, at 380.

[3] 18 Colo. App. 49 (1902).

In *Edde v. Columbia University*,[4] the plaintiff sought a court order to compel the university to reinstate him as a certified candidate for the degree of Doctor of Philosophy. The faculty committee had rejected his original dissertation; when the plaintiff refused to submit a revised dissertation, the rejection of his candidacy became final. Having reviewed the facts, the Supreme Court of New York held that "[T]he University was under no legal compulsion to continue the candidacy of a person whose dissertation had been disapproved and who refused to revise it for further consideration."[5] Further, the decision said, it would be unwise for the court to substitute its opinion on the merits of the dissertation for that of those selected by the university for the purpose of determining the quality of a student's work.

Thus the courts display a reluctance to interfere in the internal decisions of colleges and universities unless there is apparent unfairness.

In any case, students are cautioned to acquaint themselves with statements printed in the college bulletin and student regulation manuals that bear on the school's academic and social policies. A comprehensive knowledge of the regulations will enable the student to understand what he can expect of the institution and what the institution requires in return. Furthermore, one who knows his rights is least likely to be deprived of them. If, after careful reading of the catalog, a prospective student finds the rules and regulations too restrictive, he may wish to consider a college or university where the atmosphere is more compatible with his own views of student life.

Although it is apparent that institutions have wide discretion to refuse course credit, to dismiss students for academic deficiency, and to deny degrees, their prerogatives in this area are not without limits. Colleges and universities must act with a sense of responsibility and be consistent in applying rules for academic evaluation. This point was made as early as 1891 in *People ex rel. Cecil v. Bellevue Hospital Medical College*.[6] The Supreme Court of New York held that the faculty's decision arbitrarily to dismiss Cecil, a medical student who

[4]8 Misc. 2d 795, affirmed 6 A.D.2d 780 (1957).
[5]*Ibid.*, at 796.
[6]14 N.Y.S. 490 (1891), affirmed 128 N.Y. 621.

had completed the requirements for his degree, without a stated reason was not a valid exercise of discretion. The court commented:

This [college] cannot take the money of a student, allow him to remain and waste his time (because it would be a waste of time if he cannot get a degree) and then arbitrarily refuse when he has completed his term of study to confer on him that which they have promised, namely, the degree. . . . It is nothing but a wilful violation of the duties which they have assumed.[7]

In a later case the courts granted relief to a student who had acted in reliance on his faculty advisor's incorrect interpretation of certain academic regulations. In the case of *Blank v. Board of Education of the City of New York*,[8] the Supreme Court of that state held that ". . . the dean of faculty may not escape the binding effect of the acts of his agents performed within the scope of their apparent authority, and the consequences that must equitably follow therefrom."[9]

The same general legal principles involved in cases concerning graduation apply to grades and awarding academic course credit. If it can be shown that a grade is arbitrary and capricious and not a fair evaluation of a student's academic performance, then the courts will grant relief. In *Connelly v. University of Vermont and State Agriculture College*,[10] the court recognized the principle that if an instructor declared he would not give the student a passing grade, regardless of the quality of the student's work, this would amount to bad faith and capriciousness. Another case dealing with academic credits earned by the student held that the school must allow them to be transferred regardless of the reasons for the student's dismissal. In *Strank v. Mercy Hospital of Johnstown*,[11] the student violated one of the school's rules. She was dismissed, and her request to transfer two years of nursing credits was denied. The decision of the nursing school was predicated on a catalogue stipulation that stated that

[7] *Ibid.*, at 490.
[8] 51 Misc. 2d 724 (1966).
[9] *Ibid.*, at 730.
[10] 244 F. Supp. 156 (Vt. 1965).
[11] 383 Pa. 54 (1955).

no transfer credit would be given for students dismissed for an infraction of any rule. The State Supreme Court of Pennsylvania, in its decision, favored the student and ordered the hospital nursing school to issue the earned credits.

CONCLUSION

When issues involving grades, course credit, and graduation arise, the courts will be hesitant to interfere with institutional decisions unless it can be clearly shown that the decision was arbitrary, capricious, or made in bad faith. Although the courts are less reticent than formerly in this area, the reader must realize that in these cases it is always the duty of the person challenging the institution's decision to prove bad faith. This is often a difficult undertaking.

The responsible institution should provide procedures to review decisions made concerning grades, academic credits, and graduation. When a student is dissatisfied with a decision bearing upon his scholastic performance, he should have ready access to the review procedures. Furthermore, academic standards and grading criteria should be made known with a high degree of clarity, both in the school catalogue and during the first meeting of each course.

Connelly v. The University of Vermont
and State Agricultural College

United States District Court, D. Vermont, 1965
244 F. Supp. 156.

GIBSON, District Judge:

. . . The substance of the plaintiff's complaint is as follows: He is a third year student at the defendant's College of Medicine, and during the months of March through June of 1964, he was enrolled in a twelve week course in pediatrics-obstetrics. He states that due to illness he missed a portion of the course from May 11 to June 7, 1964, that he made up this lost time from July 1 to July 16, 1964, and that he believes his grades prior to his illness were 82 and 87 in the pediatrics and obstetrics parts of the course respectively. He further states that on July 17, 1964, he was advised that he failed the pediatrics-obstetrics course and could not advance to his fourth year by reason of having failed 25 per cent or more of the major courses of his third year, this under a rule of the College of Medicine. The plaintiff then petitioned the College's Committee on Advancement for permission to repeat his third year's work. His petition was denied and he was subsequently dismissed from the school. He alleges that his teacher during the period from July 1 to July 16, 1964, decided early in the period "that he would not give plaintiff a passing grade in said pediatrics-obstetrics course regardless of his prior work in the Spring and regardless of the quality of his work in said make up period." The plaintiff alleges that his work was of passing quality, and that his dismissal was wrongful, improper, arbitrary, summary and unjust. He prays that it be recinded by the mandate of this court. . . .

The important question presented here is whether plaintiff's allegation that his instructor in the make up period from July 1 to July 16, 1964, failed him without proper attention to the quality of his work and on the basis of a decision made prior to the completion by plaintiff of his pediatrics-obstetrics course, states a cause of action under Rule 56, F.R.C.P. This Court is of the opinion that it does to a limited extent.

Where a medical student has been dismissed for a failure to attain a proper standard of scholarship, two questions may be involved; the first is, was the student in fact delinquent in his studies or unfit for the practice of medicine? The second question is, were the school authorities motivated by malice or bad faith in dismissing the student, or did they act arbitrarily or capriciously? In general, the first question is not a matter for judicial review. However, a student dismissal motivated by bad faith, arbitrariness or capriciousness may be actionable.

. . . [S]chool authorities [have] asbolute discretion in determining whether a student has been delinquent in his studies, and to place the burden on the student of showing that his dismissal was motivated by arbitrariness, capriciousness or bad faith. The reason for this rule is that in matters of scholarship, the school authorities are uniquely qualified by training and experience to judge the qualifications of a student, and efficiency of instruction depends in no small degree upon the school faculty's freedom from interference from other noneducational tribunals. It is only when the school authorities abuse the discretion that a court may interfere with their decision to dismiss a student. . . .

The rule of judicial nonintervention in scholastic affairs is particularly applicable in the case of a medical school. A medical school must be the judge of the qualifications of its students to be granted a degree; courts are not supposed to be learned in medicine and are not qualified to pass opinion as to the attainments of a student in medicine. *People ex rel. Pacella v. Bennett Medical College*, 205 Ill. App. 324. In the instant case, the plaintiff Connelly alleges on information and belief

. . . that, on the basis of his work in the Pediatrics-Obstetrics course during the Spring of 1964, he either received, or, in the alternative, should have received a passing grade therein and that his work in said course was comparable to and in many instances superior to the work of other students who received a passing grade in that course.

Whether the plaintiff should or should not have received a passing grade for the period in question is a matter wholly within the jurisdiction of the school authorities, who alone are qualified to make such a determination. The subject matter of this count of the complaint is not a subject for judicial review and this count of the complaint fails to state any claim for which relief can be granted.

However, to the extent that the plaintiff has alleged his dismissal was for reasons other than the quality of his work, or in bad faith, he has stated a cause of action. He has alleged

. . . that the agent of defendant's College of Medicine who taught plaintiff from July 1 to July 16, 1964, decided early in said period that he would not give plaintiff a passing grade in said Pediatrics-Obstetrics course regardless of his prior work in the Spring and regardless of the quality of his work in said make up period.

The plaintiff has also alleged that the action of defendant in dismissing him was "summary and arbitrary." The allegation that the plaintiff was failed by an instructor who made up his mind to fail him before he completed the course is equivalent, in this Court's opinion, to an allegation of bad faith, arbitrariness, and capriciousness on the part of the said instructor, and if proven, this Court would be justified in affording the plaintiff appropriate relief.

It follows from this that the defendant's motion for summary judgment under Rule 56, F.R.C.P. must be denied. Since there appear to be genuinely disputed issues of fact as to whether the defendant's conduct was arbitrary, capricious or in bad faith, the plaintiff is entitled to have these issues tried before this Court.

It should be emphasized that this Court will not pass on the issue of whether the plaintiff should have passed or failed his pediatrics-obstetrics course, or whether he is qualified to practice medicine. This must and can only be determined by an appropriate department or committee of the defendant's College of Medicine. . . . Therefore, should the plaintiff prevail on the issue of whether the defendant acted arbitrarily, capriciously or in bad faith, this Court will then order the defendant University to give the plaintiff a fair and impartial hearing on his dismissal order.

. . . The case is to be set for hearing on the limited issue of whether the defendant University acted arbitrarily, capriciously, or in bad faith in dismissing the plaintiff.

University of Miami et al. v. Militana
District Court of Appeal of Florida, 1966
184 So.2d 701

PER CURIAM:

The appellant, University of Miami, was the respondent in the circuit court to a petition for mandamus. The petition of the appellee sought an order directing the University of Miami to promote the petitioner to the fourth year class of the School of Medicine and to enroll him during the ensuing school year. The trial judge entered an order awarding the peremptory writ in the terms described, and this appeal is from that judgment. . . .

Militana was admitted to the University's School of Medicine in the fall of 1959. At the end of his first academic year, the Promotions Committee recommended that he be promoted to the second year on probation. After the second year, the Promotions Committee recommended that he be given the opportunity of repeating the second year. Militana repeated the second year and was promoted to the third year. At the conclusion of his third year, Militana had a cumulative grade point average of 1.92—a grade point average of 4.00 is equivalent to an "A." The Promotions Committee recommended that he be promoted to the fourth year on probation, subject to additional satisfactory work and re-examination in obstetrics-gynecology and pediatrics. During the summer of 1963 Militana successfully completed the required work in pediatrics. He did not successfully complete the work in obstetrics and gynecology. At the conclusion of his work in the summer of 1963, the Executive Committee of the School of Medicine dismissed him for academic failure. . . .

The bulletin or catalogue of the School of Medicine of the University of Miami for September 1959, under which the appellant entered that school, contains the following provision for promotion of medical students.*

In general, a scholastic accomplishment of 1.0 (C average) is necessary for promotion for one year to the next, but promotion is finally determined by the Promotions Committee. In addition to the grade average, the Promotions Committee considers such qualities as attitude, industry, and general conduct in making its recommendations. This Committee may

*Under the present system a 2.0 average is equivalent to a "C."

recommend promotion, promotion on probation, repetition of a course or of a year's work, or dismissal. In case the Committee recommends the repetition of a year's work for a first year student, the student must be readmitted by the Admissions Board in competition with other applicants before he may repeat the work. Students promoted on probation shall have the conditions of probation described by the Promotions Committee and shall be so notified by the Office of the Dean.

The operation of a private college or university is touched with eleemosynary characteristics. Even though the public has a great interest in seeing these institutions encouraged and supported, they are operated as a private business. This being true, the college may set forth the terms under which it will admit and subsequently graduate students who subject themselves to the rules, regulations and regimen of the college. It is generally accepted that the terms and conditions for graduation are those offered by the publications of the college at the time of enrollment. As such, they have some of the characteristics of a contract between the parties, and are sometimes subject to civil remedies in courts of law.

The provisions quoted above clearly vest a discretionary power in the faculty of the School of Medicine as to the promotion of students. The provision is not against public policy because many years of experience have demonstrated the ability of the private colleges and universities of this Country to carry out their assumed task of educating their students.

Having concluded that, under the private contract here sought to be accomplished, promotion from one class to another is clearly within the discretion of the faculty (Promotion Committee) of the School of Medicine at the University of Miami, we must hold that the peremptory writ was erroneously awarded because mandamus cannot be used to control an exercise of discretion.

Appellee seeks to avoid this conclusion by proofs in the record and argument in this Court that the School of Medicine of the University of Miami is the recipient of funds from the public treasury of the United States and from the public treasury of the State of Florida for the education of the students therein enrolled. Even though the opinion in *John B. Stetson University v. Hunt*, 88 Fla. 510, 102 So. 637 (1925), indicated that a private institution may become subject to legislative regulation when it receives appropriations from the public treasury, the record before us will not support the appellee's conclusion that the public source of these funds has changed the character of the University or created any additional rights in the students. Nor do we find that the determinative principles of law are different for private and for public institutions and colleges. If the performance of an act or duty involves the exercise of discretion and no clear legal duty is shown, mandamus will not lie. . . .

The order granting peremptory writ of mandamus is reversed.

4

CONFIDENTIALITY OF
STUDENT RECORDS

Seldom does a school year pass in which a college or university
is not faced with the question of its responsibility regarding the confidentiality of student records. There are requests for information
from government agencies, prospective employers, and parents, to
name a few. Occasionally the inquiries take on national significance.
Within recent years, requests for information regarding student
activities by certain governmental organizations have caused wide
outbursts of indignation and posed important legal questions. The
House Un-American Activities Committee in 1966 issued subpoenas
to individual college and university presidents ordering them to
produce membership and officer lists of anti-Vietnam campus organizations.[1] In Pennsylvania, the Higher Education Assistance Agency
of that state requested colleges and universities throughout the nation
to report the names of all Pennsylvania students who were either
dismissed or convicted of a felony as a result of their attempts to
disrupt classes or other campus activities. The Agency threatened
to cut off state aid to all Pennsylvania students at any institution
that refused to comply with the request.[2] And the Committee on

[1] *The New York Times*, November 14, 1966, p. 16.

[2] *The Corporation of Haverford College, et al v. Reecher, et al*, Civil Action No. 70-2411,
filed in the U. S. District Court for the Eastern District of Pennsylvania.

Internal Security of the U.S. House of Representatives conducted a survey concerning the honorariums paid to radical speakers. 177 colleges and universities were requested to provide information to the Committee. The data sought included names of the speakers, sponsorship, and costs.[3]

Of course such inquiries or surveys have a national significance and often create dramatic debates on the confidentiality of student records. But no less significant are the day-to-day decisions made on college campuses regarding the release of data assembled in the normal course of a student's college career.

Herein lies a major question that involves students, faculty, and administrators alike. Decisions regarding the extent of confidentiality to be given student records cannot but affect the personal and professional life of the individual student. It is a vital matter that does not always receive sufficient administrative attention or student concern.

The degree of confidentiality to be given to student records is not altogether clear. In certain instances the law recognizes the right of the individual(s) to keep personal information confidential. State statutes and court rulings, however, sharply curtail the exercise of this right, which is by no means applicable to all information, documents, or records in general.

This legal recognition of guaranteed confidence is founded upon two principles of law. The first is an individual's right of privacy. The second is recognition that certain relationships carry with them a privilege of secrecy. Examples of the latter are the information exchanged between an attorney and client, and between a husband and wife. The privileged communication between such special parties is based on public policy, which recognizes that, in order to encourage full and free disclosure between these special parties, the law must grant the liberty of silence.[4]

The right to privacy constitutes legal recognition that an individual has prerogatives to safeguard certain facets of his personal

[3]Report of Inquiry Concerning Speakers' Honoraria at Colleges and Universities, Report No. 91-1732, Union Calendar No. 834, U. S. House of Representatives, Committee of Internal Security, December 14, 1970. Also see *Hentoff, et al v. Ichord, et al*, Civ. Action No. 3028-70, U. S. District Court for the District of Columbia.

[4]Charles T. McCormick, *Evidence* (St. Paul, Minn.: West Publishing Co., 1954), p. 152.

life from invasion by others. The courts, in honoring this right, will prohibit an incursion on the private aspects of a person's life. The right of privacy issue, however, has received slight legal recognition or consideration in cases involving college students.

On the other hand, the rule of privileged communication offers some support for limiting the extent of the use that can be made of student records. Before going further, it is essential to distinguish between two types of privilege, absolute and qualified. An absolute privilege is one in which the recipient cannot disclose to anyone information obtained as a result of the relationship. Only a legislature can give an absolute privilege, and the relationships covered can vary from state to state. For instance, in addition to the attorney-client and husband-wife privilege, there can be privilege for the physician-patient and the priest-penitent. Other relationships may also be covered, but they are unimportant in the context of this discussion.

The protection granted by absolute privilege may be waived. Ordinarily, it is only the communicating party that may do the waiving. For example, it is the client, not the attorney, who has the right to waive the confidential protection. But there may be a slight variation of this rule when it comes to the husband-wife relationship. In some jurisdictions, it has been held that the privilege belongs to both, and therefore it is not waivable by just one of the parties.

Qualified privilege is one that permits the disclosure of information, without the consent of the maker of the statement, to certain individuals for specific purposes only. A college disclosing information regarding a student's financial responsibility to a bank represents an illustration of a legitimate disclosure.

Revealing information under a qualified privilege is not without restriction. There are certain standards that must be met before student information can be released. A school may generally divulge information from its records under the following conditions:

1. The information must be requested and not voluntarily offered.
2. It must be given to a person having a real interest in the matter and a need to know.
3. The information given shall not exceed the scope of the request.

4. It must be given in good faith, and not with intent to damage the individual.[5]

Who determines the standards of confidentiality to be followed by a university? On this point there appear to be few legal decisions or statutes imposing restrictions on colleges and universities. Of course, where an absolute privilege applies, i.e., infirmary records based on a physician-patient relationship, there is no question that there must be nondisclosure. Beyond this certainty, there is wide legal latitude available to the individual institution. A great deal will depend on its sensitivity to the legal rights of its students.

In the absences of adequate legal precedent establishing standards of confidentiality for student records, one is required to look to other sources. Several educational associations have drafted guidelines covering this area. One of the best was issued by the American Council on Education in 1967.[6]

The statement represents the Council's reaction to the House Un-American Activities Committee's attempt to subpoena membership lists of campus organizations known to oppose the war in Southeast Asia. The document recognized the obligation of educational institutions to cooperate with committees of the Congress, but at the same time emphasized an equal obligation "to protect students from unwarranted intrusions into their lives and from hurtful or threatening interference in the exploration of ideas and their consequences that education entails." It went on to point out that the maintenance of student records, especially those bearing on personal belief and organizational affiliation, creates a personal and confidential relationship. More specifically, the Council suggested the release of nothing more than the student's name, dates of his registered attendance, nature of any degree granted, and the dates on which the degrees were conferred, in the absence of consent of the student. Any further information should be released, barring consent, under "only irresistable legal compulsion." The statement of the

[5]Robert B. Meigs, "The Confidential Nature of Student Records," *National Association of College and University Attorneys* (Transcript—Second Annual Conference), June 1962, p. 16.

[6]Statement on Confidentiality of Records by the American Council on Education, Washington, D. C., July 7, 1967.

American Council on Education recommended that in cases in which a particular individual is suspected of violating the law or has information sought by an investigatory body, the person involved should be approached directly and that authorized ways be used to secure the information. There is no need, the Council believes, to require the college or university to act as an informer in such matters.

Four recommendations were made to institutions of higher learning to guide their future actions. In summary form, they are:

1. Mindful of the principle that student records should be held in a relationship of confidentiality between the student and institution, each college and university should formulate and firmly implement clear policies to protect the confidential nature of student records. . . .
2. When demands which challenge the fundamental principle of confidentiality are made for information about students' beliefs or associations, no response, beyond the reaffirmation of the principle, should be made without consultation with attorneys. . . .
3. Institutional policy should pay proper respect to the interest of research and scholarship to insure that the freedom of inquiry is not abridged. . . .
4. Colleges and universities should discontinue the maintenance of membership lists of student organizations, especially those related to matters of political belief or action. . . .[7]

The *Model Code for Student Rights, Responsibilities, and Conduct* covers the matter of student records quite thoroughly. It provides:

Student Records

35. The privacy and confidentiality of all student records shall be preserved. Official student academic records, supporting documents, and other student files shall be maintained only by full-time members of the institution staff employed for that purpose. Separate files shall be maintained of the following: academic records, supporting documents, and general educational records; records of discipline proceedings; medical and psychiatric records; financial aid records.

36. No entry may be made on a student's academic record and no document may be placed in his file without actual notice to the students. Publication of grades and announcement of honors constitute notice.

[7]*Ibid.*

37. Access to his records and files is guaranteed every student subject only to reasonable regulation as to time, place, and supervision.
    A. A student may challenge the accuracy of any entry or the presence of any item by bringing the equivalent of an equitable action against the appropriate person before the [appropriate] judicial body. . . .
38. No record may be made in relation to any of the following matters except upon the express written request of the student:
    A. Race;
    B. Religion (unless an institution clearly and publicly states a religious preference);
    C. Political or social views; and
    D. Membership in any organization other than honorary and professional organizations directly related to the educational process.
39. No information in any student file may be released to anyone except with the prior written consent of the student concerned or as stated below:
    A. Members of the faculty with administrative assignments may have access for internal educational purposes as well as routinely necessary administrative and statistical purposes.
    B. The following data may be given any inquirer: school or division of enrollment, periods of enrollment, and degrees awarded, honors, major field, and date.
    C. If an inquiry is made in person or by mail, the following information may be given in addition to that in Subsection B: address and telephone number, date of birth, and confirmation of signature.
    D. Properly identified officials from federal, state and local government agencies may be given the following information upon express request in addition to that in Subsections B and C: name and address of parent or guardian if student is a minor, and any information required under legal compulsion.
    E. Unless under legal compulsion, personal access to a student's file shall be denied to any person making an inquiry.
40. Upon graduation or withdrawal from the institution, the records and files of former students shall continue to be subject to the provisions of the Code of Conduct.[8]

Students should not be misled by these suggested guidelines. Although they represent a statement of the highest standards to

[8]Committee on Student Rights and Reponsibilities, Law Student Division, American Bar Association, 1969.

be observed in matters of student record disclosure, they are no more than recommendations. A California case provides a good example of a decision that ignored the guidelines issued earlier by the American Council of Education. In *Eisen v. Regents of the University of California*,[9] a student at Berkeley challenged the University's right to make public the purpose and names of the officers of student organizations. The facts of the case show that a University rule requires each campus organization to submit a statement of purpose and the names of its officers before formal recognition of the organization would be granted. In 1966 a citizen filed a suit against the University officials asking for the disclosure of the names of officers and purposes of all registered organizations. The University granted the citizen's request and adopted a policy that registration statements be open to public inspection. A lower court ruled against the student plaintiff, and on appeal, the ruling was affirmed. It was the finding that public policy requires such disclosure. The compelling interest of the public in obtaining information, the decision stated, outweighs any minimal infringement of an individual's right. The court observed that First Amendment rights do not require anonymity. It added that such disclosure maintains "the integrity of the extracurricular aspects of the educational process at a public university."

The court opinion said:

. . . just as the people of the state have a right to know how their elected officials conduct the public business, they are entitled to know the identity of responsible officers of organizations that are granted the privileges of becoming campus organizations and using the public property and facilities of the University.

A determining factor in cases such as *Eisen* may very well have been the purpose for which the information is sought. If Eisen sought disclosures of a more personal nature and for a different purpose, he might have met greater judicial resistance. Another California case,[10] decided in 1963, did suggest some restriction on student record disclosure. It held that there was a reasonable basis for college authorities to restrict the circulation of a student's transcript of scholastic

[9]75 Cal. Rptr. 45 (1969).
[10]*People v. Russell*, 29 Cal. Rptr. 562 (1963).

records. But a later decision, *Cole v. Trustees of Columbia University*,[11] found that where there was only a remote danger of government action that might be directed against the students on the basis of information in the records, a university could release the contents of the students' files to a U.S. Senate Committee pursuant to a subpoena.

In both *Eisen* and *Cole*, the information released was requested for more than a private or personal purpose. Apparently, requests by police, government agencies, corporations, and others acting in the public's interest will be honored without legal restriction on an institution.

Of course a student can always release his own records. He may do it specifically by granting permission or impliedly by applying for employment, knowing that inquiries will be made about his college record. There have been cases in which courts have ordered the release of such personal records to students after they have been denied access to them by university officials.[12] A father's petition for the right to inspect his son's school record was turned down by the Board of Education, but granted by the state court. The decision observed:

Absent constitutional, legislative or administrative permission or prohibition, a parent is entitled to inspect the records of his child maintained by the school authorities as required by law.[13]

Needless to say, although there are no recorded cases on the point, parents of students over twenty-one would have no such right. In general, though, colleges usually cooperate with parents seeking specific information, regardless of the student's age.

A corollary problem arising from the confidentiality of records principles occurs when a student seeks to investigate the contents of his own university file. For example, such a file may contain letters of recommendation for graduate study, personal evaluations by instructors and administrative personnel, etc. The issue is whether the student may legitimately request that this material be made available to him. If so, will the institution be successful in securing

[11]300 F. Supp. 1026 (S.D.N.Y., 1969).

[12]*Morris v. Smiley*, 378 S.W. 2d 149 (Texas, 1964).

[13]*Matter of Van Allen v. McCleary*, 27 Misc. 2d 81, 93 (S. Ct. Nassau County, 1961).

candid and complete evaluations in the future if the writers are concerned that their communications will be made available for perusal by the student? It is our opinion that if such file material bears upon a decision affecting the student, he has the right to be informed and given an opportunity to refute it. In these cases, the inconvenience to the institution is outweighed by the student's right to know under the Fourteenth Amendment.

In addition to the general Fourteenth Amendment protection, state institutions are generally subject to the so-called "right to know" laws applicable to public records. These enactments typically provide that governmental records shall be available for inspection and copying and set up specific procedures to accomplish it. The student should consult the particular law in his state if such a problem should arise.

CONCLUSION

Despite the dearth of clearly defined legal rules, it can be said that confidentiality of student records is a principle that is generally recognized by colleges and universities. There are serious questions for which answers are not available, however. It is certain that every individual, student and non-student, has a right of privacy. The absolute privilege limited to special confidential relationships affords a barrier of protection unless waived by the communicating party. Less definite are the parameters provided by a qualified privilege. Generally, although information contained in the student's file cannot be released to the public, a wide number of individuals can have access to it if they show a sufficient reason for their interest. At least this much can be said: teachers, administrators, parents, and public officials, while engaged in their official duties, and prospective employers have the right of full or partial access to a student's file. In addition, the records are always subject to lawful subpoena.

Such extensive right of access, although not totally condemned, is contrary to the statements of confidentiality drafted by the American Council on Education and the Law Student Division of the American Bar Association. These organizations suggest a sharp limitation to the information that can be made available on general inquiry. The limitations would include releasing data relating only to a student's school or college, periods of enrollment, degrees awarded, honors awarded, and major field of study.

These guidelines provide a reliable source for an institution's conduct in this area. Nevertheless, they do not have the authority of legal precedent or statute, and students must be kept ever mindful of this fact. Their value lies in their persuasive power to convince institutions to amend their policies on the confidentiality of student records to reflect a standard that will afford a student greater protection regarding those facets of his life that he wishes to keep private.

Eisen v. The Regents of the University of California

California Court of Appeal, First District, 1969
75 California Reporter 45

TAYLOR, Associate Justice:

. . . The basic facts are not in dispute. Plaintiff was a law student at the University's Berkeley campus and an officer of a student organization engaged in the advocacy of dissident ideas. This organization was fully qualified as a student organization "registered" by the University. An organization that has complied with registration procedures and attained the status of a "registered" student organization, is entitled to several privileges on campus, including the use of University facilities for meetings, fund raising, recruiting participants, posting and distributing literature, as well as the privilege of inviting non-University speakers to address campus meetings. As a condition of "registration" the University required that the organization submit to the appropriate campus officer a statement of its purpose and the names of its officers. Plaintiff's name was submitted under this requirement.

In October 1966, a member of the public, Patricia Atthowe, filed a suit against the officers of the Berkeley campus praying, inter alia, the disclosure of the names of the officers and stated purposes of all student campus organizations "registered" for the spring semester of the 1965-1966 academic year. On October 17, 1966, the University made public a letter written to Patricia Atthowe indicating that on advice of its counsel, the University would allow her to examine the documents containing the information she demanded.

On October 25, the University adopted a policy "that registration statements filed with the University by student organizations are records open to inspection by University students and staff and members of the public." This action ensued, and a temporary restraining order issued. After a hearing, the trial court found "that public policy as framed within the law of this State requires disclosure of the subject records, such public policy being dominant and controlling to the right of associational privilege," and entered its orders dissolving the temporary order and dismissing the action.

The parties agree that the University's rule-making powers and its relationship with its students and student organizations are subject to federal constitutional guarantees; and that ideas, no matter how unpopular or erroneous in their dissemination, including the formation of groups and associations to advance such ideas are fully protected by the First Amendment. . . .

[W]e deal with the issue presented in the constitutional framework of whether here, the University's policy of annexing limited disclosure conditions to the privilege of becoming a registered campus organization entitled to use campus facilities, are justified by a sufficient state interest to outweigh the alleged impairment of plaintiff's constitutional rights. . . .

Plaintiff argues that he is entitled to a constitutional right of anonymity and that the disclosure of the "registration" statements to inspection by members of the public has a deterrent effect on his rights of free speech and association. . . .

The question here presented is whether the right of the People of this state to know the identity and responsible officers of student organizations that may be using the publicly financed and owned campus facilities of the University is a sufficient state interest to warrant the indirect infringement of plaintiff's First Amendment rights. . . .

[J]ust as the People of the state have a right to know how their elected officials conduct the public business, they are entitled to know the identity and responsible officers of organizations that are granted the privileges of becoming campus organizations and using the public property and facilities of the University. Nor can it be successfully argued that the protection of plaintiff's First Amendment rights requires complete anonymity. The U.S. Supreme Court has held that First Amendment freedoms are not violated by legislation requiring "a modicum of information" of lobbyists (*United States v. Harriss*, 347 U.S. 612, 613-617, 74 S.Ct. 808, 98 L.Ed. 989). . . .

We question the consistency of plaintiff's assertion of a right to keep anonymous his relationship as an officer of the organization (a relationship and responsibility he presumably sought and assumed voluntarily) in the absence of any immediate and direct threats of physical or other danger. . . . Thus, it can reasonably be inferred that the disclosure sufficient to identify the organization and the officers responsible for its activities is not . . . repugnant to First Amendment freedoms.

Nor . . . can it be said that the identification requirement of the University's policy and the disclosure of this limited information to a member of the public would unduly deter the freedom of expression of dissident organizations and their officers. In fact, it appears well designed to promote that freedom of expression in a manner consistent with the University's interest in insuring the orderly enjoyment of its facilities together with the public's right to ascertain the identity of organizations and the responsible officers who are using public property. The Regents' policy here in issue is like a time, place and manner regulation of free speech enacted to maintain the integrity of the extracurricular aspects of the educational process of a public university. . . .

Impairments of First Amendment rights are "balanced" by determining whether there is a reasonable relationship between the impairment and a subject of overriding and compelling state interest. There can be no doubt that disclosure requirements may impair rights of free speech and association and that First Amendment rights are primarily intended to protect minority views. We conclude, however, . . . that here the compelling interest of the public in being able to ascertain the information contained in the registration statement outweighs any minimal infringement of plaintiff's First Amendment rights.

It may be contended that even though the overriding purpose is legitimate and substantial, the purpose can be achieved by means more narrow than the University's policy in question. The only information made available to the public is the purpose of the organization and the names of its officers found on the registration statement submitted to the appropriate campus officer. We think this modicum of information is well within . . . express limits. . . .

Cole v. The Trustees of Columbia University
United States District Court, S.D. New York, 1969
300 F. Supp. 1026

TENNEY, District Judge:

This is a motion brought on by the plaintiffs, Columbia University Chapter of Students for a Democratic Society, and certain of its members, suing on behalf of other individuals and/or organizations similarly situated, for an order, pursuant to Rule 65(a), (b) of the Federal Rules of Civil Procedure, restraining the defendants, The Trustees of Columbia University (hereinafter referred to as "the Trustees"), from disclosing, revealing or delivering any books, records, reports, correspondence, membership lists, associational information or other documents specified in a subpoena duces tecum served upon the Trustees by the Permanent Subcommittee on Investigations of The Committee on Government Operations of the United States Senate. The Trustees, rather than risk contempt of Congress, for failure to comply with this subpoena issued by the Subcommittee, intend to release the material requested on June 5, 1969.

The underlying cause of action seeks a declaratory judgment, pursuant to Title 28, United States Code, Section 2201, declaring the subpoena duces tecum served upon Columbia University unconstitutional and void, and a permanent injunction prohibiting the Trustees from complying therewith. . . .

Briefly, as background to the present litigation, Students for a Democratic Society (hereinafter referred to as "SDS") is an unincorporated association consisting of young people whose views may be considered to rest at the left of the political spectrum. They seek a radical, democratic program, the methods of which embody their vision, that is, a vision of a democratic society ". . . where at all levels the people have control of the decisions which affect them and the resources on which they are dependent." . . . In furtherance of the Society's objectives, its chapters and members have often been the focal point of the expression of opposition to certain foreign and domestic policies of the United States Government. In this respect, and in accordance with its aims and purposes, the organization has both directly and indirectly participated in campus disorders which have resulted from the spread of student unrest. . . .

Turning to the issue which I find to be of paramount importance in reaching my determination herein, that is, the doctrine of separation of powers, a district court must exercise extreme caution not to encroach upon legislative functions, and, accordingly, must not assume jurisdiction over any matter which does not amount to a justiciable controversy. It is apparent from the present posture of this case that the parties presently seeking the injunction are neither threatened by a taking of property belonging to them nor with any infliction of punishment, such as Congressional citation for contempt. This Court will not attempt to protect the plaintiffs from a danger yet unknown. Needless to say, the judiciary would construct an insurmountable barrier in the path of every Congressional investigating committee if it were to allow the bona fides of the legislative authorization to be challenged in a court of law by any person who could conceivably be affected by the testimony elicited or documents produced at a Senate hearing.

Even assuming, *arguendo*, that the questions presented herein were ripe for litigation, it would be incumbent upon the plaintiffs, prerequisite to obtaining a hearing, to make a substantial factual showing that the Congressional investigation is unrelated to any proper legislative function in that it is beyond the powers conferred upon Congress by the Constitution or that in authorizing the investigation by the Subcommittee, the Senate failed to spell out the Committee's jurisdiction and purpose with sufficient particularity to insure that compulsory process was only in furtherance of the legislative purpose. Absent a substantial factual showing in this regard, it is not the business of a district court to investigate the bona fides underlying legislative motives. Having thoroughly considered the papers submitted by the plaintiffs in this cause, it is apparent that they contain mere conclusory allegations unsupported by any factual elaboration. . . .

5

SPEAKER PROGRAMS
AND STUDENT PRESS

Students, as citizens of a college community, possess certain basic
rights and freedoms. Equally, as in the larger society, they have
responsibilities to that community. As a result, there is the ever-
present question about the limits of the academic and personal freedoms of the student as a campus citizen. Within this classification of
basic rights, two areas stand out, for they require continual institutional clarification and judicial definition. They involve speaker
programs and the student press.

The First Amendment of the United States Constitution pro-
hibits the abridgement of "the freedom of speech or of the press."[1]
Also by interpretation of the Fourteenth Amendment, the U. S.
Supreme Court makes the same prohibition application to the states.[2]

Since 1791, when the Bill of Rights was ratified, the courts
have been faced with interpreting the intent of the Founding Fathers
in guaranteeing free speech and free press. These rights and the
limits placed upon them to assure an equal balance of maximum

[1]Amendment I, United States Constitution: "Congress shall make no law re-
specting an establishment of religion or prohibiting an establishment of religion or
prohibiting the free exercise thereof; or *abridging the freedom of speech or of the press*;
[emphasis added] or the right of the people peaceably to assemble, and to petition
the Government for a redress of grievances."

[2]*Gitlow v. New York*, 268 U.S. 652 (1925).

65

liberty within the limits of restraint to assure an orderly society often raise delicate questions. Colleges and universities have proven to be a fruitful source for cases dealing with these controversial problems.

SPEECH

Speaker bans are instituted by campus authorities in an attempt to control the content of speeches and limit the appearance of "unacceptable" personalities on campus. When the ban is challenged in court it will be upheld *only* for serious reason. Anyone, including colleges and universities, imposing such a restriction is confronted with justifying the action by clear and convincing proof of its constitutionality. Nearly always, the principle applied in cases banning campus speakers is the "clear and present danger" doctrine. The burden is on the school authorities to show that, if not banned, the speech will prove to be detrimental to the orderly operation of the institution. They must convince the court that there will be advocacy of ". . . willful destruction or seizure of property of the university, forcible disruption of educational functions, invasion of lawful rights of officials, faculty or students, or some other campus disorder of violent nature."[3] Another essential point is that the danger must represent a present or future harm. Belief in a doctrine advocating a particular action is not sufficient. A person may not be penalized for belief only; he must do something more, such as acting on that belief or exhorting others to act on that belief. When weighing the danger involved, the court will assess the environment in which the speech is to be delivered. It will consider the personality of the speaker, the current political temper, the content of the speech, the composition of the audience, and the nature of the forum.

Without a clear and present danger, an institution cannot implement a speaker ban. This does not imply that a college does not have the prerogative to exercise discretion in the selection of speakers. It can establish standards of minimum qualifications of expertise and intelligence to assure a contribution to the educational program. Speaker regulations may require certain procedures to be followed by a recognized student or faculty group before official approval is

[3]*Molpus et al. v. Fortune,* 311 F. Supp. 240 (N.D. Miss., W.D., 1970).

given. Valid requirements may include reasonable advance notice, information concerning the date, time, and location, anticipated audience size, and a brief statement concerning the subject matter of the talk. Of course, rules pertaining to campus speakers constitute a prior restraint upon freedom of speech and freedom of assembly; therefore, they must provide an ascertainable standard of conduct. Courts will rule them invalid if their terms are so vague that persons of average intelligence must guess at their meaning and differ as to their application.[4]

Regulations may not ban political or unpopular moral, social, or religious speeches.[5] They cannot prevent the appearance of an individual because of membership in an organization or because the speaker may have associated with others who advocate destructive or dangerous action.[6] Furthermore, the criminal record of a speaker has proven to be an unjustifiable ground for excluding a student-invited speaker from the campus.[7] Nor can the facilities of an institution be withheld because a speaker may be controversial or hold views unacceptable to the college. Once facilities are made available for a general speakers' program, they must be open to all unless valid procedural steps have not been followed or the speech falls within the scope of a clear and present danger.[8]

Once the institution's authorization has been received for the appearance of a guest speaker, there are continuing responsibilities for the sponsoring group. Although members of a student organization ought not be held accountable for any illegal actions of the speaker, they do become liable in disciplinary actions where there was a knowledge of a probable violation of the law, and such violation does occur. On the other hand, guest speakers when appearing on the campus are always accountable for their own actions with or without student involvement, under the general law, and thereby subject themselves to legal proceedings when their behavior justifies such an action.

[4]*Smith v. University of Tennessee*, 300 F. Supp. 777 (E.D. Tennessee, N.D., 1969).
[5]*Dickson v. Sitterson*, 280 F. Supp. 486 (M.D. North Carolina, 1968).
[6]*Stacy v. Williams*, 306 F. Supp. 963 (N.D. Mississippi, W.D., 1969).
[7]*Brooks v. Auburn University*, 296 F. Supp. 188 (M.D. Alabama, E.D., 1969).
[8]*Buckley v. Meng*, 230 N.Y.S.2d 924 (1962).

PRESS

Student publications, as do other published material, often provoke First Amendment questions concerning the constitutional limits placed upon the printed word. Generally, rules controlling other forms of student expression apply equally to publications. College newspapers, literary and humor magazines, academic periodicals, yearbooks, and campus exhibitions qualify for freedom of the press protection. This protection does not entirely rule out regulatory measures, which, when imposed, must be reasonable and must avoid infringement on legally recognized rights of free expression.[9] A college or university may exercise its regulatory powers to avoid institutional liability, or, in unusual cases, to meet a clear and present danger to the school.[10]

Censorship of a student publication is totally inconsistent with First Amendment freedoms. Censorship can take the form of administrative or faculty review, limitations placed on distribution, or termination of funds. No matter what methods are used, the courts in a preponderant number of cases have ruled against censorship of any kind.

The reasons given for supporting censorship of student publications are numerous. Obscene material or language are often considered by school officials to be sufficient justification to forbid the preparation or distribution of a publication. Most courts would find this an insufficient cause for institutional action.[11] In state schools, criticism of a political nature often strikes too close to home and meets unpopular reaction. The resulting discomfort created by the criticism leads to outcries for banishment of the student editor or the shutdown of the publication, or both. Courts have little tolerance for such reaction and rule consistently in favor of the students.[12] Cases involving criticism of school officials in a student newspaper are similarly dealt with by the courts.[13]

[9]*Dickey v. Alabama State Board of Education*, 273 F. Supp. 613 (M.D. Alabama, N.D., 1967).

[10]*Scoville v. Board of Education of Joliet Township High School District 204*, 425 F.2d 10 (1970).

[11]*Antonelli v. Hammond*, 308 F. Supp. 1329 (D. Massachusetts, 1970).

[12]*Dickey v. Alabama State Board of Education, supra* Note 9.

[13]*Sullivan v. Houston Ind. School District*, 307 F. Supp. 1328 (S.D. Texas, 1969).

Although censorship is the issue most often involved in cases involving student publications, several others merit consideration. What limits may be placed upon advertising copy that appears in a college or university newspaper? Restrictive advertising policies are not looked upon with kindness by judges. Editorial advertisements are permissible as long as they do not "attack an institution, group, person or product."[14] Advertisements of a political nature cannot be refused merely because the school authorities see the function of the newspaper as publishing only school-related topics.[15] Despite these rulings, there is some question as to whether unrestricted advertising is allowed.

Since the liberalization of abortion laws, for example, many college newspapers have been carrying "ads" for abortion referral services. This practice has come under criticism on both legal and moral grounds. A look at the action taken in Connecticut on this issue will prove informative. In Connecticut, abortion advertisements have been withdrawn from newspapers in several private and state institutions of higher education after the criminal statutes were called to their attention:

Encouraging the commission of abortion. Any person who, by publication, lecture or otherwise or by advertisement or by the sale or circulation of any publication, encourages or prompts to the commission of the offenses [miscarriage or abortion] or who sells or advertises medicines or instruments or other devices for the commission of any of said offenses except to a licensed physician or to a hospital approved by the state department of health, or who advertises any so-called monthly regulator for women, shall be fined not more than five hundred dollars or imprisoned not more than one year or both.[16]

The constitutional issue of this matter has not as yet been litigated.

Students should consult the statutes of their state for the most reliable information on this subject. In those jurisdictions where abortion is legalized, there should be no problem in advertising an abortion referral service. In these states, however, caution would

---

[14]*Lee v. Board of Regents of State Colleges,* 306 F. Supp. 1097 (W.D. Wisc., 1969).

[15]*Zucker v. Panitz,* 299 F. Supp. 102 (S.D. New York, 1969).

[16]Connecticut General Statutes Section 53-31.

suggest the extra step of consulting the state statutes to be sure and thereby to avoid legal penalty.

Another problem that has recently caused a flurry of court activity regarding student publications is the underground newspaper. The decisions that have been rendered on this point clearly indicate, despite a few opposing cases, that underground newspapers are a valid activity. Schools may not prohibit them nor penalize students responsible for their publication unless they violate the accepted standards applicable to other published materials. Students have every right to prepare and circulate a newspaper prepared independently and distribute it on or off the school grounds.[17] Most authorities would extend this right to include leaflets.[18]

Such publications are, in most cases, the result of student reaction to what they consider oppressive regulatory practices of the school. Many college newspapers, in order to free themselves from rules promulgated by authorities to control the newspaper, are considering independent operation. The Yale *Daily News*, the Harvard *Crimson*, and the Cornell *Daily Sun* have been independent for years. The advantages of such an arrangement are self-evident. By cutting ties with the college, the newspaper is free from supervision, and the danger of censorship is eliminated.

Other considerations, however, require close scrutiny. Besides the usual financial problems involved in an independent venture, there are legal ramifications. By operating outside the structure of the institution, the paper and its personnel are individually subject to lawsuit. Facts and accusations appearing in each issue will require scrupulous checking. Lawsuits for libel become a real possibility. A *caveat* to students considering a change to independent status for their paper is most appropriate. All the ramifications of such a move should be considered carefully, especially the legal questions that are apt to arise.

Regardless of its dependent or independent status, a student newspaper may be liable for publishing articles that bring harm to a person's reputation or business. No matter what the reason for causing the injury—carelessness or recklessness—the newspaper may have

---

[17]*Eisner v. Stamford Board of Education*, 314 F. Supp. 832 (D. Conn., 1970).
[18]*Jones v. Tennessee State Board of Education*, 407 F.2d 834 (1969).

to answer for damages in libel cases. A newspaper policy of reporting on the basis of demonstrable fact will go a long way in avoiding charges of libel, and the policy should be strictly enforced by the editors and school regulation.

As another matter of policy, it might be advisable for the publication to provide a right to reply by any individual who has been adversely affected by an article or editorial comment. Although such a right is not legally recognized, it does embody the essentials of free press.[19]

CONCLUSION

The concept of encouraging students to participate in the unrestricted transmission of knowledge is a cherished one dating back to the age of Greece. The courts, steeped in their own custom of respect for the free flow of ideas, have proven to be a champion for protecting this tradition. Nowhere is this more obvious than in the judicial decisions dealing with speaker bans.

The right of free press applies to student publications. Unless the printed material fails the clear and present danger test or is illegal as a matter of law, there should be no infringement. Students have a wide latitude to print their views and observations. Even when they are ill-tempered and in bad taste, the protection of the First Amendment applies. Justice Douglas has said:

Strongly abusive utterances or publications, not just merely polished urbane pronouncements of dignified people, enjoy First Amendment protection.[20]

Nevertheless, there are recognized limitations that can be imposed on student publications. Institutional measures may be taken to guarantee responsible journalism, but not censorship or control.

[19]Report of the American Bar Association, Commission on Campus Government and Student Dissent, p. 15, 1970.

[20]*Jones v. Tennessee State Board of Education*, 397 U.S. 31, 33 (1970).

Smith v. University of Tennessee
United States District Court E.D. Tennessee, N.D., 1969
300 F. Supp. 777.

ROBERT L. TAYLOR, Chief Judge:

Plaintiffs seek to enjoin officials of the University of Tennessee from enforcing rules which prohibit students from inviting as speakers for university sponsored programs persons who do not meet certain standards. . . .

Plaintiffs are primarily students and faculty of the defendant university. . . .

The University of Tennessee is a state owned and operated institution of higher learning. . . . Defendants A. D. Holt, Charles H. Weaver and Robert Gordon are respectively the President, Chancellor and Vice-Chancellor for Student Affairs of the University of Tennessee.

Throughout the period of the operative facts in this suit and until the present the University has had in force guidelines for student invitations to speakers. Those guidelines appear in the student handbook as follows:

A. *Choice of Speaker*

An invitation to a speaker who is to be sponsored by a student organization must be approved by the appropriate officers and faculty-alumni advisers to that organization and registered with and approved by the Dean of Students as meeting the following criteria:

(1) The speaker's competence and topic shall be relevant to the approved constitutional purpose of the organization;

(2) There is no reason to believe that the speaker intends to present a personal defense against alleged misconduct or crime which is being adjudicated in the courts;

(3) There is no reason to believe that he might speak in a libelous, scurrilous or defamatory manner or in violation of public laws which prohibit incitement to riot and conspiracy to overthrow the government by force. . . .

C. *Appeal or Referral*

In addition to the criteria in (A) above, the University Faculty Committee must consider the general question of whether the invitation and its timing are in the best interests of the University.

Issues is one of two officially sanctioned lecture series at the University of Tennessee. Unlike *Man and his Environment*, the other lecture series, *Issues* is presently composed solely of student members. Both *Issues* and *Man and his Environment* are financed through the Student Activities and Service Fee which is assessed quarterly upon all full-time university students to defray the cost of a long list of student activities and services. *Issues* operates on an annual budget of $12,000.00 and *Man and his Environment* on an annual budget of $9,000.00.

As one of the speakers for its fall quarter program *Issues* had selected Dick Gregory, the Negro civil rights activist who at the time was a candidate for President of the United States. After the invitation was initially approved by the administrative officials as required by the handbook rules, the contract for Mr. Gregory's appearance was duly forwarded by *Issues* to defendant Gordon for execution by the appropriate financial officers of the University.

On or about September 10, 1968, officers of *Issues* were informed by Chancellor Weaver, in the presence of Gordon, that Mr. Gregory would not be permitted to appear on the University campus as a student invited speaker. Two days later, Chancellor Weaver issued a statement entitled "Freedom of Speech on the Campus" in which he said that the administration fully supported unhindered freedom of speech by faculty, students and speakers invited by the academic departments. He expressed the view that student speaker invitation programs constituted in effect a separate university of questionable educational benefit, and which created problems in maintaining the freedom of speech of the faculty.

The *Issues* program issued an invitation to Dr. Timothy Leary to speak on February 27, 1969, as a part of winter quarter *Issues* schedule. Leary is known primarily as an advocate of the use of the hallucinogenic drug LSD. On February 4, Chancellor Weaver announced that the University administration had refused finally to issue a contract for the appearance on campus of Dr. Leary.

During its October meeting the Board of Trustees adopted a resolution which directed the chancellors of the individual campuses of the university to develop speaker policies which must be submitted to and approved by the Trustees before becoming effective. At its February meeting, the Board set up a committee to recommend a new speakers policy for the consideration of the Board at its June gathering.

The *Issues* program has scheduled an appearance by Leary for May 6, 1969; but the Acting Vice Chancellor for Student Affairs has declined to approve the invitation. Plaintiffs allege present and future injury in the nature of a violation of their First and Fourteenth Amendment rights because of the refusal of the defendants to allow Gregory and Leary to speak. They contend that the policy as announced in the student handbook is unconstitutionally broad and vague. Temporary and permanent injunctive relief are sought and in addition a declaratory judgment that the current policy of the University is unconstitutional. . . .

This case involves the balancing of rights of students and teachers protected by the First and Fourteenth Amendments of the Federal Constitution and of the officials of the University of Tennessee to control and regulate public speaking on University property. If possible, the rights of the parties should be reconciled so as to avoid the destruction of the rights of either.

The First Amendment provides in pertinent part:

> Congress shall make no law . . . abridging the freedom of speech, . . . or the right of the people peaceably to assemble, and to petition the Government for a redress of grievances.

The right of freedom of speech is applicable to States under the Due Process Clause of the Fourteenth Amendment. . . .

The First Amendment protection of free speech extends to listeners. . . .

Further, it has long been recognized that in carrying out their primary mission of education, state owned and operated schools may not disregard the constitutional rights of students. . . .

It is conceded that the Board of Trustees and administrative officials of state supported universities have the right to enforce rules and regulations governing the appearance of guest speakers. No one has the absolute, unlimited right to speak on a university campus; however, when the university opens its doors to visiting speakers, it must follow constitutional principles if it seeks to regulate those whom recognized groups may invite. The fundamental question in this lawsuit is whether the applicable constitutional principles require that the university's regulations on student-invited speakers not be vague or broad. . . .

Unlike laws which penalize speech after it is uttered, as in the case with slander, the university's regulations on speakers have the effect of preventing speech before it is spoken. Prior restraints on speech come to the courts with a heavy presumption against their constitutional validity. . . .

When a statute or regulation either forbids or requires the doing of an act in terms so vague that men of common intelligence must necessarily guess at its meaning and differ as to its application, it violates the due process clause of the Fourteenth Amendment because of vagueness. Stricter standards of vagueness apply where the statute potentially inhibits speech. Regulations may not withstand constitutional scrutiny which are so broad that they threaten speech which is protected by the First Amendment.

Guideline No. 1 in the student handbook requires the guest speaker's competence and topic to be relevant to the approved constitutional purpose of the organization. Who is to judge the competence and the topic? What standards are to be used in so judging? Isn't competence, like real estate values, a relative term? Do people always agree as to whether a person is competent or incompetent? The term is so broad and vague that an administrator could, if he chose to do so, act as an unrestrained censor of the expression of ideas with which he does not agree.

Guidelines Nos. 2 and 3 provide in effect that there shall be no reason to believe that the speaker intends to present a personal defense against alleged misconduct or crime which is being adjudicated in the courts and no reason to believe that he will speak in a libelous, scurrilous or defamatory manner or in violation of public laws which prohibit incitement to riot and conspiracy to overthrow the government by force. Who is to judge these matters and what standards shall be used in finding the answers?

The final and Fourth Guideline provides that the University Faculty Committee in addition to the criteria to be considered in Guidelines 1, 2 and 3 must consider the general question of whether the invitation and its timing are in the best interests of the University. Any speaker could be debarred from the campus if it were determined that he was invited at the wrong time under this guideline. This vests in the administrative officials discretion to grant or withhold a permit upon criteria unrelated to proper regulation of school facilities and is impermissible.

It was the belief of our forefathers that censorship is the enemy of freedom and progress. We have lived by this principle since it was written by them in our Federal Constitution, and it has proved beneficial to the nation and its citizens. The interchange of ideas and beliefs is a constitutionally protected necessity for the advancement of society.

The Court is constrained to hold that the plaintiffs are entitled to declaratory relief. The University has made its policy to allow recognized student groups to invite speakers and to make university facilities available to both speaker and audience. The regulations by which the University denies permission for the appearance of speakers which students have selected are required by the Constitution to be clearly and narrowly worded. The existing regulations which appear in the Student Handbook do not satisfy those requirements.

The defendants are responsible citizens who occupy high positions in state government. We believe that they will abide by the declaration of this Court that the current policy of the University of Tennessee is not in accord with plaintiffs' First Amendment rights because the standards fixed for the selection of outside speakers are too broad and vague. For that reason injunctive relief is not granted at this time but plaintiffs may renew their application at an appropriate time if it becomes necessary.

Saunders v. Virginia Polytechnic Institute

United States Court of Appeals, Fourth Circuit, 1969
417 F. 2d 1127.

WINTER, Circuit Judge:

On the facts of this case we must decide how a conflict between a student's First Amendment right to register dissent and the power of a state university to control activities on its campus is to be resolved. The district court denied the student, Thomas J. Saunders (Saunders), a preliminary injunction against the refusal of Virginia

Polytechnic Institute (VPI) to readmit him, and dismissed his complaint. Saunders has appealed. . . .We conclude that the order of the district court should be reversed. . . .

In the spring of 1969, Saunders was a student at VPI. Through two and one-half years at the school he had maintained an unusually high academic average and an unblemished disciplinary record. His campus activities in opposition to the war in Vietnam had been articulate and persistent. On April 28, 1969, he resigned from VPI because of his heavy involvement in extra-curricular activities. Simultaneously, he applied for readmission for the fall quarter which began in September 1969. On May 6, VPI informed Saunders that he had been accepted for readmission in the fall quarter and that he would receive the "formal notice of readmission" sometime in August. It required the return of a signed form to signify acceptance of readmission. Saunders signed and returned the form on May 7.

On May 23, VPI announced that General William G. Westmoreland, Army Chief of Staff, would be the speaker at the commissioning exercises for the VPI reserve officer training corps contingents. These exercises were to be held on June 7 during VPI's commencement week-end. The "Committee for Peace in Vietnam," a campus group of which Saunders was a member, planned an anti-war demonstration at these exercises. The demonstration took place. It was peaceful and did not disrupt the ceremonies. . . .

Saunders was warned both before and during the demonstration that his participation would violate school policy. The warnings referred to a policy contained in a document entitled "Procedures to be Observed in the Event Disruptive Activities Develop on Campus." This document set forth the following rule:

If there are any individuals who are not matriculated students or staff of the University participating in picketing, demonstrations or similar activities . . . on . . . campus, these individuals will immediately be asked to leave . . . . In the event such individuals refuse to leave when requested, they will immediately be subject to arrest.

These warnings to Saunders proceeded, of course, on the administrative determination that he was not a "matriculated student" and hence, was not within the group from which peaceful picketing, demonstrations or similar activities would be tolerated. Despite the warnings, Saunders persisted in his participation.

Subsequently, VPI denied Saunders readmission, solely on the ground that he had violated school policy by taking part in the demonstration. No person who engaged in the demonstration was arrested, and no other student was disciplined in any way.

VPI is a state-supported and state-owned institution. Therefore, Saunders contends that VPI's action contravened his First Amendment rights. He urges us to hold, *inter alia*, that, short of violent or disruptive activities, he and all other members of the public had the right to be present on the VPI campus to register an antiwar protest. VPI responds to this claim with the assertion that it has the power to exclude from the campus persons whose presence would be detrimental to its well-being. It also contends that "matriculated students" have the right to engage in campus demonstrations and since Saunders was not a matriculated student, he was properly denied readmission for having participated in the peaceful, non-obstructive demonstration of June 7.

The fundamental nature of all First Amendment rights requires an evaluation of VPI's contention that it had the power to discipline Saunders because he was not a "matriculated student" while it admits that it lacks like authority over the other students who participated in the demonstration. The argument we find unpersuasive. A student's freedom to express peaceful dissent on campus is more than a privilege; . . . it is a basic right guaranteed by the First Amendment. A state university is powerless to restrict or deny it as long as it is not obstructive or disruptive. . . .

At the time that the peaceful, orderly and nondisruptive demonstration took place, Saunders' status was not different to any marked degree from that of the students whose rights of expression were respected. Of course, Saunders either had not received, or did not have the right to receive, grades for the expiring semester because he had resigned. But his right to attend classes in the fall was neither greater nor less than those who demonstrated with impunity. Even students who had completed the semester were required to apply for readmission to the fall session. Like Saunders, their right to be admitted had not yet vested because they could have been denied readmission for a violation of VPI rules. Whatever the significance to VPI between a "matriculated student" and one in Saunders' position for its own administrative purpose, we deem the difference too insubstantial to deny Saunders his right of free expression.

We reject VPI's argument that it must restrict participation in campus demonstrations to "matriculated" students for the reason that the conduct of persons who are not members of its academic community is not subject to its control because its disciplinary procedures cannot be used to deter the possibility of disruption. Saunders was as much a part of the academic community as those whose participation went undisciplined, and the attempted denial of readmission to Saunders shows that in a proper case VPI is not powerless. In any demonstration which transcends the proper exercise of free speech, we have no doubt that VPI has full access to non-campus police to quell the disturbance or disruption.

We do not reach VPI's additional argument that when outsiders participate in campus demonstrations there is necessarily a greater potential for disruption than is characteristic of demonstrations limited to students. The argument is inapplicable to Saunders, because from past association and tentative future acceptance, he was no less a member of the academic community than the other students whose rights were respected.

We hold, therefore, that VPI's denial of readmission to Saunders violated his First Amendment right, that the disciplinary action must be set aside and Saunders reinstated. . . .

Reversed and remanded.

Dickey v. Alabama State Board of Education et al.

United States District Court, M.D. Alabama, N.D., 1967
273 F. Supp. 613.

JOHNSON, Chief Judge:

. . . During the early part of the 1966-67 school year, Gary Clinton Dickey, while a full-time student at Troy State College, was chosen as an editor of the Troy State College student newspaper, The Tropolitan. It appears that Dickey was an outstanding student, as he was also chosen as editor-in-chief of the Troy State College

literary magazine; was copy editor of the college's annual student
yearbook, and was editor-in-chief of the student handbook. He was
also a member of a national honorary journalism fraternity.

In early April 1967, Dr. Frank Rose, President of the University of Alabama, came under attack by certain Alabama state legislators for his refusal to censor the University of Alabama student
pubiication, "Emphasis 67, A World in Revolution." "Emphasis
67," as published for the University of Alabama, served as the program for a series of guest speakers and panel discussions held in
March at the University of Alabama. . . . The theme of the "Emphasis" program was a "World in Revolution. . . ." After public
criticism by certain Alabama legislators, Dr. Rose, in the exercise
of his judgment as President of the University of Alabama, took a
public stand in support of the right of the University students for
academic freedom. Criticism of Dr. Rose for this position by certain
state legislators became rather intense. The newspapers widely pub-
licized the controversy to a point that it became a matter of public
interest throughout the State of Alabama.

Editor Dickey determined that the Troy State College newspaper, The Tropolitan, should be heard on the matter. He prepared
and presented to the faculty adviser an editorial supporting the
position taken by Dr. Rose. He was instructed by his faculty adviser
not to publish such an editorial. . . . Dickey then went directly to
the president of the college, Ralph Adams, who also determined that
the editorial could not be published. . . . [T]he basis for the denial
of Dickey's right to publish his editorial supporting Dr. Rose was a
rule that had been invoked at Troy State College to the effect that
there could be no editorials written in the school paper which were
critical of the Governor of the State of Alabama or the Alabama
Legislature. The rule did not prohibit editorials or articles of a lauda-
tory nature concerning the Governor or the Legislature. The rule has
been referred to in this case as the "Adams Rule." The theory of the
rule, as this Court understands it, is that Troy State College is a
public institution owned by the State of Alabama, that the Governor
and the legislators are acting for the owner and control the purse
strings, and that for that reason neither the Governor nor the Legislature could be criticized. . . . Dickey, as editor of The Tropolitan,
. . . and, acting against the specific instructions of his faculty adviser

and the president of the college arranged to have—with the exception of the title, "A Lament for Dr. Rose"—the space ordinarily occupied by the editorial left blank, with the word "Censored" diagonally across the blank space. In addition to this conduct, Dickey mailed the censored editorial to a Montgomery newspaper. All parties in this case concede that the editorial is well written and in good taste. However, the evidence in this case reflects that solely because it violated the "Adams Rule," Dickey's conduct, in acting contrary to the advice of the faculty adviser and of President Adams, was termed "willful and deliberate insubordination." This insubordination is the sole basis for his expulsion and/or suspension.

It is basic in our law in this country that the privilege to communicate concerning a matter of public interest is embraced in the First Amendment right relating to freedom of speech and is constitutionally protected against infringement by state officials. The Fourteenth Amendment to the Constitution protects these First Amendment rights from state infringement, . . . and these First Amendment rights extend to school children and students insofar as unreasonable rules are concerned. Boards of education, presidents of colleges, and faculty advisers are not excepted from the rule that protects students against unreasonable rules and regulations. This Court recognizes that the establishment of an educational program requires certain rules and regulations necessary for maintaining an orderly program and operating the institution in a manner conducive to learning. However, the school and school officials have always been bound by the requirement that the rules and regulations *must be reasonable*. . . . Regulations and rules which are necessary in maintaining order and discipline are always considered reasonable. In the case now before this Court, it is clear that the maintenance of order and discipline of the students attending Troy State College had nothing to do with the rule that was invoked against Dickey. As a matter of fact, the president of the institution, President Adams, testified that his general policy of not criticizing the Governor or the State Legislature under any circumstances, regardless of how reasonable or justified the criticism might be, was not for the purpose of maintaining order and discipline among the students. On this point, President Adams testified that the reason for the rule was that a newspaper could not criticize its owners, and in the case of a state institution the owners were to be considered as the Governor and the members of the Legislature.

With these basic constitutional principles in mind, the conclusion is compelled that the invocation of such a rule against Gary Clinton Dickey that resulted in his expulsion and/or suspension from Troy State College was unreasonable. A state cannot force a college student to forfeit his constitutionally protected right of freedom of expression as a condition to his attending a state-supported institution. State school officials cannot infringe on their students' right of free and unrestricted expression as guaranteed by the Constitution of the United States where the exercise of such right does not "materially and substantially interfere with requirements of appropriate discipline in the operation of the school." . . . The defendants in this case cannot punish Gary Clinton Dickey for his exercise of this constitutionally guaranteed right by cloaking his expulsion or suspension in the robe of "insubordination." The attempt to characterize Dickey's conduct, and the basis for their action in expelling him, as "insubordination" requiring rather severe disciplinary action, does not disguise the basic fact that Dickey was expelled from Troy State College for exercising his constitutionally guaranteed right of academic and/or political expression.

It is . . . ordered that the defendants immediately reinstate Gary Clinton Dickey as a student in Troy State College, commencing September 11, 1967.

Antonelli v. Hammond

United States District Court, D. Massachusetts, 1970
308 F. Supp. 1329

GARRITY, District Judge:

. . . In the spring of 1969 plaintiff Antonelli was duly elected by the student body of Fitchburg State College to serve for one year as the editor-in-chief of the campus newspaper. At the start of the fall semester in September 1969 Antonelli changed the name of the paper from *Kampus Vue* to *The Cycle*. The change in name was indicative of a change in policy and format. While *Kampus Vue's* focus had been primarily on student news and events on campus, *The Cycle* sought to explore and comment upon areas of broader social and political impact.

The Cycle is not financially independent. It depends on an allocation of a portion of revenues derived from compulsory student
activity fees. In accordance with Mass. G.L. c. 73, § 1B, these fees
and any receipts from the student activities themselves are retained
in a revolving fund to be expended "as the president of the college
may direct in furthering the activities from which the fees and receipts were derived . . . ." Prior to the present dispute, the publication costs and other bills of the student newspaper at Fitchburg
State College had been consistently paid from this fund. Without
this money the campus newspaper cannot be published on a regular basis.

On September 21, 1969, an article entitled "Black Moochie"
written by Eldridge Cleaver and originally appearing in *Ramparts
Magazine*, Vol. 8, No. 4., October 1969, was included in the material
for Vol. 1, No. 3, of *The Cycle* submitted to Raymond Plante, the
paper's usual printer. Mr. Plante, whose daughter is a student at
the college, strenuously objected to the theme of and four-letter
words generously used in the text of "Black Moochie." He refused
to print the article, preferring to smash his presses first, and he tele-
phoned President Hammond to inform him of the content of the
edition which the students were asking him to print. . . . President
Hammond had not been pleased with the change in the focus and
format that previous issues of *The Cycle* had brought to the campus
newspaper. On this occasion and thereafter the defendant indicated
to the plaintiff and others that he felt morally obligated to use his
powers over the allocation of funds for student activities under G.L.
c. 73, § 1B, to see that the money was spent properly and to prevent its expenditure on the publication of such "trash" as "Black
Moochie." He stated that therefore he would not consider paying
for articles like "Black Moochie" and would refuse to allow future
editions of *The Cycle* to be published unless he or someone acting
with his authority approved of all the matter to be included in the
newspaper prior to its being printed.

In order that some form of student publication continue during
the pendency of these proceedings, and under protest, plaintiff agreed
to cooperate with an advisory board of two faculty members, Drs.
Greene and Quigley, who were appointed by the defendant to exercise their judgment as to the "responsible freedom of the press" in
the student newspaper. Under President Hammond's plan, funds

from student fees would not be forthcoming for future issues until the issues were approved by the advisory board.

The primary function of the advisory board is to pass on the acceptability of material intended to be published in *The Cycle* and to prevent the printing of articles which the administration feels are not fit for the campus newspaper. No guidelines of acceptability were established and no standards limit the discretion of the two faculty members as they pass judgment on the material submitted to them. No procedure was designed whereby the reasonableness or validity of a board decision might be tested or reviewed.

Prior to the present controversy, the officials at Fitchburg State College had left control over the content of the campus newspaper entirely to the student editors. Only with the attempted publication of "Black Moochie" did President Hammond feel it necessary to interpose administrative control in the form of the advisory board.

On November 7, 1969, plaintiff repudiated his agreement to cooperate with the advisory board and he and the entire editorial board submitted their resignations. This action was announced in the one issue of *The Cycle* published under the control of the advisory board, Vol. 1, No. 4. It was prompted by disputes with the two faculty members as to the newspaper's financial responsibility and budgetary mechanics.

Although the conflict leading to the resignations did not concern material submitted for publication and although the board neither rejected nor censored in any way the material actually proposed for the one issue printed under its auspices, the controversy over censorship still colored the relationship of the student editors and representatives of the administration. . . .

The Cycle has not been published since the announcement of the resignations on November 7. The office of editor-in-chief will have been officially vacant since December 17, 1969. Although he would have to be reelected by the student body, Antonelli testified that he would be willing to run again and serve as editor-in-chief if the advisory board were eliminated. . . .

Turning to the merits of the plaintiff's claim to freedom from censorial supervision by the advisory board, we note first the absence of any express limitation on the board's powers to review and approve. All manner of intended publication must be submitted; there is no exception, so there is nothing that does not come within the censor's purview. Therefore, the powers actually conferred could presumably be used, without change in form or need for expansion, to achieve complete control of the content of the newspaper. However, there is no indication of any intention to go beyond excising obscenity, and in any event, for purposes of this case, we must construe the powers conferred upon the advisory board by the defendant in the narrowest light possible, i.e., censorial only over the obscene. This is essential because the plaintiff claims freedom from an obligation to submit anything for prior approval.

No matter how narrow the function of the advisory board, it constitutes a direct previous restraint of expression and as such there is a "heavy presumption against its constitutional validity." *Bantam Books, Inc. v. Sullivan*, 1963, 372 U.S. 58, 70, 83 S.Ct. 631, 639, 9 L.Ed. 2d 584.

It is true that the advisory board proposes to suppress only obscene writings and that obscenity does not fall within the area of constitutionally protected speech or press. . . . However, the manner and means of achieving the proposed suppression are of crucial importance. . . . Whenever the state takes any measure to regulate obscenity it must conform to procedures calculated to avoid the danger that protected expression will be caught in the regulatory dragnet. . . .

Nothing of the sort is included in the system devised by the defendant for passing upon the contents of *The Cycle*. It lacks even the semblance of any of the safeguards the Supreme Court has demanded. The advisory board bears no burden other than exercising its judgment; there is no appeal within the system from any particular decision; and there is no provision for prompt final judicial determination. . . . Indeed, final responsibility rests with two faculty members, serving at the pleasure of the defendant, who so far as the evidence showed are wholly unfamiliar with the complex tests of obscenity established by the Supreme Court in cases such as *Roth v. United States*, 1957, 354 U.S. 476, 77 S.Ct. 1304, and the *Memoirs, Ginzburg* and *Mishkin* cases, 1966, 383 U.S. 413-518, 86 S.Ct. 975, 942, 958, 16 L.Ed.2d 1, 31, 56. Accordingly, the court concludes that the defendant's establishment of the advisory board is prima facie an unconstitutional exercise of state power.

If the advisory board of *The Cycle* is to withstand constitutional challenge, it can only be because there is something either in the institutional needs of a public university or in the nature of a newspaper funded from student activity fees that justifies a limitation of free expression and thereby permits an exercise of state power plainly unwarranted if applied to the press generally. . . .

No such justification has been shown in the instant case. Obscenity in a campus newspaper is not the type of occurence apt to be significantly disruptive of an orderly and disciplined educational process. Furthermore, assuming that a college administration has a sufficient educationally oriented reason to prevent the circulation of obscenity on campus, there has been no showing that the harm from obscenity in a college setting is so much greater than in the public forum that it outweighs the danger to free expression inherent in censorship without procedural safeguards. If anything, the contrary would seem to be true. The university setting of college-age students being exposed to a wide range of intellectual experience creates a relatively mature marketplace for the interchange of ideas so that the free speech clause of the First Amendment with its underlying assumption that there is positive social value in an open forum seems particularly appropriate.

There is an added element in the present case: the expenses of publishing *The Cycle* are payable by the college from funds received from compulsory student activity fees. Does this circumstance significantly alter either the rights of the students or the powers of the college president over the campus press? We think not. Contrary to the defendant's contention, Mass. G.L. c. 73, § 1B, does not make him ultimately responsible for what is printed in the campus newspaper. Under that section, student activity fees "shall be expended as the president of the college may direct in furthering the activities from which the fees and receipts were derived; . . ." This imposes no duty on the president to ratify or to pass judgment on a particular activity. The discretion granted is in the determination whether the funds to be expended actually further the activities to which they are intended to be applied. Once that determination has been made, the expenditure is mandatory.

We are well beyond the belief that any manner of state regulation is permissible simply because it involves an activity which is a part of the university structure and is financed with funds controlled by the administration. The state is not necessarily the unrestrained master of what it creates and fosters. Thus in cases concerning school-supported publications or the use of school facilities, the courts have refused to recognize as permissible any regulations infringing free speech when not shown to be necessarily related to the maintenance of order and discipline within the educational process. . . .

Because of the potentially great social value of a free student voice in an age of student awareness and unrest, it would be inconsistent with basic assumption of First Amendment freedoms to permit a campus newspaper to be simply a vehicle for ideas the state or the college administration deems appropriate. Power to prescribe classroom curricula in state universities may not be transferred to areas not designed to be part of the curriculum.

Accordingly, since (a) there is no right to editorial control by administration officials flowing from the fact that *The Cycle* is college sponsored and state supported, and (b) defendant has not shown that circumstances attributable to the school environment make necessary more restrictive measures than generally permissible under the First Amendment, the court holds and declares that the prior submission to the advisory board of material intended to be published in *The Cycle*, in order that the board may decide whether it complies with "responsible freedom of the press" or is obscene, may not be constitutionally required either by means of withholding funds derived from student activity fees or otherwise.

6

DEMONSTRATIONS

Probably no single phenomenon has been more unsettling to the academy in recent years than the emergence of mass student demonstrations and protests covering a variety of real or imagined wrongs and running the gamut from quality of food in the cafeteria to the war in Indochina. The philosophy and rationale behind such tactics need not concern us here. What is significant is that a vocal minority of students have for one reason or another concluded that meaningful change, reform, or debate are not possible within the structure of the existing educational bureaucracy. Their alternative is to seek the accomplishment of their ends by extra-legal means. The reactions to such movements by the university range from repression to capitulation, and often include a good deal of confusion. These new movements of protest have tested not only the viability of the educational complex, but also the responsive capacity of the American legal system.

FREE SPEECH AND THE CLEAR
AND PRESENT DANGER DOCTRINE

Before attempting any analysis of the legal responses to student demonstrations, it is necessary to consider the development of some of the limitations upon the First Amendment freedoms of speech and assembly.

A student of American constitutional law is often inclined to associate Justice Oliver Wendell Holmes with the most significant interpretations of the Bill of Rights protections of freedom of speech. One of his best known decisions was that of *Schenck v. United States*,[1] which is often cited as the first clear-cut statement of what has become known as the "clear and present danger test." The *Schenck* case arose out of a conviction of conspiracy to violate the espionage act of June 15, 1917. The specific allegations included the obstruction of the recruiting and enlistment service of the United States while this country was engaged in World War I. In particular, the defendants circulated anti-war material to draftees. The court affirmed the conviction of the defendants, with Justice Holmes writing the majority opinion. He stated:

. . . the character of every act depends upon the circumstances in which it is done. . . . The most stringent protection of free speech would not protect a man in falsely shouting fire in a theatre and causing a panic. . . . The question in every case is whether the words used are used in such circumstances and are of such a nature as to create a clear and present danger that they will bring about the substantive evils that Congress has a right to prevent. It is a question of proximity and degree.[2]

A week later in *Frohwerk v. United States*,[3] Justice Holmes elaborated on this view. This case also concerned convictions under the espionage act and the court ruled that ". . . The First Amendment while prohibiting legislation against free speech as such cannot have been, and obviously was not, intended to give immunity for every possible use of language."

Much confusion remained as to the applicability of this language in particular cases, however. For example, in *Abrams v. United States*,[4] the court affirmed by a 7 to 2 vote a conviction for disseminating literature "obviously intended to provoke and to encourage resistance to the United States in the war." Justices Holmes and Brandeis dissented, arguing that conviction under the clear and present danger test was proper only when there was a present danger

[1]249 U.S. 47 (1919).
[2]*Ibid.*
[3]249 U.S. 204 (1919).
[4]250 U.S. 616 (1919).

of immediate evil or an intent to bring it about. Holmes and Brandeis, in the Abrams case, did not feel the facts warranted conviction under the immediate danger test. A similar result was reached in *Schaefer v. United States*,[5] with Holmes and Brandeis again dissenting. What appears to have occurred at this time was a breakdown on the court between those who adhered to the doctrine of the immediate danger test and a majority, which felt that when utterances threatened the lawful existence of government a less permissive test should be applied. This was illustrated further in the case of *Gitlow v. New York*,[6] which concerned a conviction under a New York statute that prohibited anyone from advocating, advising, or teaching the duty, necessity, or propriety of overturning government by force or violence. The court ruled that

such utterances, by their very nature, involve danger to the public peace and to the security of the state. They threaten breaches of the peace and ultimate revolution. And the immediate danger is none the less real and substantial because the effect of a given utterance cannot be accurately forseen. The State cannot reasonably be required to measure the danger from every such utterance in the nice balance of a jeweler's scale.[7]

In a prescient dissent, Justice Holmes joined with Justice Brandeis in observing that "if, in the long run, the beliefs expressed in proletarian dictatorship are destined to be accepted by the dominant forces of the community, the only meaning of free speech is that they should be given their chance and have their way."[8] This latter case illustrates the opposing views, with the majority upholding the constitutionality of statutes prohibiting utterances directed toward the overthrow of legitimate government on the grounds that such speech is within the common law standard of dangerous tendencies. This common law test was later applied in the case of *Whitney v. California*,[9] in which the majority upheld by unanimous decision a conspiracy conviction. Justices Holmes and Brandeis, however, declined to follow the majority and sought to limit the applicability of

[5]251 U.S. 466 (1920).
[6]268 U.S. 652 (1925).
[7]*Ibid.*, at 668, 669.
[8]*Ibid.*, at 673.
[9]274 U.S. 357 (1927).

the clear and present danger test, pointing out that ". . . no danger flowing from speech can be deemed clear and present, unless the incidence of the evil apprehended is so imminent that it may befall before there is opportunity for full discussion."[10]

As with many legal principles, further development followed a change in court personnel. In 1949, the Court reversed a conviction under a Chicago ordinance that prohibited speech that "stirs the public to anger, invited disputes (or) brings about a condition of unrest."[11] Justice Douglas, in the majority opinion, acknowledged that the free speech protection is not absolute, but held it is ". . . protected against censorship or punishment, unless shown to produce a clear and present danger of a serious substantive evil that rises far above public inconvenience, annoyance or unrest." The decision was on a 5-to-4 vote, with Justice Jackson pointing out in a dissenting opinion that:

many speeches, such as that of Terminiello, may be legally permissible, but may nevertheless in some surroundings be a menace to peace and order. When conditions show the speaker that this is the case, as it did here, there certainly comes a point beyond which he cannot indulge in provocations to violence without being answerable to society.[12]

The foregoing decisions indicate that, although the Court at one time applied a strict standard affirming convictions when there was a threat of danger to public peace, the standard has become more permissive; the Court upholds a conviction only when there is found to be a clear and immediate threat of public unrest. If jurists find this standard elusive in matters of national security, consider how much more difficult the task must be when the speech is uttered within the modern university, a presumed haven of free exchange. In developing a standard applicable to the university setting, the courts are not without precedent more appropriate than conspiracy indictments. The principles developed in cases involving picketing are particularly helpful.

The Supreme Court has viewed picketing as an exercise of freedom of speech and assembly that warrants Constitutional protection.

[10]*Ibid.,* at 377.
[11]*Terminiello v. Chicago,* 337 U.S. 1 (1949).
[12]*Ibid.,* at 33.

Theoretically, picketing may not be prohibited unless a clear and present danger of violence or some other substantive evil can be shown to exist. The Court adopted this view in *Thornhill v. Alabama*,[13] in which it established the principle that "the dissemination of information concerning the facts of a labor dispute must be regarded as within that area of free discussion as guaranteed by the Constitution." In view of this, the Court was of the opinion that peaceful picketing, including carrying signs, could be interfered with only if ". . . the clear danger of substantive evils aris[es] under circumstances affording no opportunity to test the merits of ideas by competition for acceptance in the market place of public opinion."[14]

Perhaps the best approach to an appraisal of the legal restrictions on university demonstrations is to consider the language and law of the immediate danger test, particularly as in the *Terminiello* case, and the standard applied to peaceful picketing. By adopting this view, a demonstration or protest becomes an exercise of free speech and as such is subject to all the protections granted by the First Amendment. University protest becomes then not a unique twentieth-century phenomenon, but the legitimate heir of a half century of legal development. We must note, however, that the benefits of this development accrue only to peaceful protest just as they accrue only to peaceful picketing. As Justice Frankfurter asserted, "utterance in a context of violence can lose its significance as an appeal to reason and become part of an instrument of force such utterance was not meant to be sheltered by the Constitution."[15]

The manner in which the Supreme Court will treat modern university protest, however, is unclear, since the Court has not made any decisions directly on the matter. An analysis of specific lower court decisions suggests there may be a pattern of development.

LEGAL DECISIONS ON COLLEGE DEMONSTRATIONS

The first significant court decision on college demonstrations begins appropriately enough in Berkeley, California. As is well known, the University of California campus in that city sustained the country's

---

[13]310 U.S. 88 (1940).

[14]*Ibid.*, at 106.

[15]*Drivers' Union v. Meadow Moore Co.*, 312 U.S. 287, 3 (1941).

first large-scale student disruptions in the spring of 1966. A review of that occurrence still leaves one puzzled as to the primary aim of the students. Impersonality of the educational bureaucracy, too much research and not enough teaching, right of free speech and assembly, and many other cries that have now become part of the conventional wisdom of academic reform were raised in the California situation. The particular situation that became the subject of judicial review was the right of students to carry signs upon which were painted epithets judged to be obscene by the administration of the University, which in turn reflected the mores of the community. This case reached the California courts as *Goldberg v. Regents of the University of California*,[16] in which the claims of the so-called filthy (free) speech movement were struck down. The courts echoed the language of earlier cases on free speech and stated that:

An individual cannot escape from social constraint merely by asserting that he is engaged in political talk or action. . . . Thus, reasonable restrictions on the freedoms of speech and assembly are recognized in relation to public agencies that have a valid interest in maintaining good order and proper decorum.[17]

Thus one of the first courts to be presented with the problem of student demonstrations indicated that as in ordinary free speech cases, the liberty was not unlimited. The *Goldberg* case set the pattern and other courts analyzing this problem have groped to find the proper balance between freedom of expression on the one hand and public order on the other. In the case of *Jones v. State Board of Education*,[18] students were suspended after involvement in demonstrations and in the preparation and distribution of literature that was characterized as highly abusive to the University administration and disruptive to University functions. The court's analysis was directed toward determining whether the conduct sought to be regulated was such as would disrupt the educational function of the institution. Upon finding in the affirmative, the court ruled that such conduct was a proper subject for control by the University. This standard is, of course, quite general, and further cases grappled with the problems

[16]57 Cal. Rptr. 463 (1967).
[17]*Ibid.*
[18]279 F. Supp. 190 (1968).

of determining exactly what conduct would tend to disrupt university functions, as well as what activities were encompassed as an institutional function.

One type of conduct that is clearly improper is the occupation of buildings or the blocking of ingress and egress to university facilities. An early case in this matter is *Buttney v. Smiley.*[19] Students at the University of Colorado had protested job recruitment by the CIA and physically prevented entrance to the interview room on campus. The pupils were suspended and sought review by the court. The court's analysis was the same as that utilized in the *Jones* case; a finding was made that job recruitment was a proper university function and the plaintiffs had, in fact, interfered with it. The court ruled that free speech does not provide protection for conduct that disrupts the operation of the institution. The blocking of ingress or egress to a university building clearly falls within this category. In this case, the court looked to the rights of persons desiring to enter the buildings, and found that they should be protected. The persons preventing lawful access to facilities were disciplined not for what they said, but for what they did.

A similar result was reached at Grambling College in Louisiana, which faced a crisis over the question of intercollegiate athletics. A large proportion of the student body felt that sports were overemphasized, and the students occupied the administration building in protest. After an unsuccessful meeting with the President, several other buildings were occupied, and the functioning of the College severely curtailed. Several students were expelled without notice and successfully applied to the court. Upon rehearing they were again suspended and once more appealed, this time on the issue of free speech rather than due process in the hearing procedure. Once again the court's analysis proceeded with reference to the functioning of the institution. The issue was not whether the students had the right to criticize the institution's athletic policies; they clearly did have this right. The issue, rather, was whether the students could assert this right by forcefully occupying buildings on the College campus and temporarily, at least, crippling its operations. The court found that such conduct was well outside the protection of the First Amendment.

[19]281 F. Supp. 280 (1968).

In addition, it stated that the College was not left with the sole alternative of expelling a large proportion of the student body, especially when the leaders of the illegal activity were definitely identified.

The previous two cases should serve to indicate that the court will not extend the protection of free speech to conduct that itself constitutes a breach of the peace or an interference with the functions of the university. This applies whether the institution is public or private. Once again, however, we have a general statement of law that is often difficult to apply in particular cases. For instance, in the case of *People v. Harrison*,[20] Michigan State University sponsored a career carnival in its student union, where representatives of potential employers could come and hold interviews. One of the booths was for the United States Marine Corps. A large group of students opposing the war in Vietnam entered the building with signs and literature and milled about in the area of the Marine Corps booth, with the result that several students who wished to get to the booth found it extremely difficult to accomplish. A college official directed the demonstrating students to leave; when they refused, he had them ejected and charged with trespass. They were convicted in the lower court and appealed. The Court of Appeals of Michigan had difficulty deciding this case. There seemed to be no question but that the purpose of the students' presence in the student union building was to inhibit the recruiting process of the marines. The court determined, however, that the activity was something less than complete obstruction and on this basis found that it was not sufficiently detrimental to constitute a violation of the local trespass ordinance. The court held that the burden of proof was upon the University to show that the ordinance had been violated, and that in this case they had failed to meet the burden.

Although courts have consistently affirmed that conduct that causes substantial disruption of university functions may render participants subject to disciplinary action, decisions have drawn a distinction between participants who plan peaceful demonstrations that later become violent and those participants who specifically plan that demonstrations should become violent. The case of *Scoggin v. Lincoln University*[21] concerned a demonstration to protest the cost

[20] 13 Mich. App. 54 (1968).
[21] 291 F. Supp. 161 (1968), U.S. District Court, W.D. Missouri, Central Division.

and quality of food in the school cafeteria. As is frequently the case, the University anticipated the demonstration and issued a statement that any such activity must be peaceful and respectful of the rights of others. As is too often the case, the demonstration escalated into a general trashing of the cafeteria. Approximately $1,500 worth of damage was incurred. After the demonstration, two of the students who had planned it were suspended. The court found no substantial evidence to support a finding that the students had planned a demonstration different from that previously authorized by the University. A distinction was drawn between the right to plan and participate in an authorized demonstration and the University's right to discipline students for unlawful conduct, including planning and knowing participation in a violent or disruptive demonstration. In order for the suspension to have been affirmed, there must have been substantial evidence that those who planned and participated in the demonstration knew and intended it to be violent.

A decision that upheld the same rule of law, but which was decided against the students, was *Siegel v. Regents of the University of California*,[22] the "People's Park" case at Berkeley. In the case, the president-elect of the University student government made a speech objecting to the University's fencing a vacant lot near the campus. He exhorted the students to camp in. The speaker's call was heeded and it subsequently became necessary to eject the students forcibly from the property, an ejection that was accompanied by considerable violence. The president-elect was placed on disciplinary probation and appealed to the court. The Federal Court in California approached the question as one of free speech, but found substantial evidence that the defendant had intentionally adopted an air of militancy in order to exhort the demonstrators to conduct that would materially and substantially disrupt the University. The court held this time that:

Illegal conduct is not protected merely because it is in part initiated, evidenced, or carried out by language. Utterance in a context of violence, involving a clear and present danger, can lose its significance as an appeal

[22]308 F. Supp. 832 (1970), U.S. District Court, N.D. California.

to reason and become part of an instrument of force and as such is unprotected by the Constitution.[23]

CONCLUSION

The foregoing case summary indicates that the issue of university demonstrations is viewed by the law in the context of free speech. This of course is in keeping with the system of American jurisprudence, which places great weight on precedent and authority. Every attorney knows that the surest way to persuade a judge is to argue that his case fits into a previously adjudicated category. Consciously or not, this is the way lawyers and judges think, and this is clearly evident in the judicial approach to college disruption. Administrators and social commentators speak of this as a unique contemporary phenomenon, whereas the courts reason from analogy to free speech principles, with particular reference to those of picketing. In this context, wide latitude will be permitted as far as speech itself is concerned. But when speech becomes action and operation of the institutions or freedom of movement on the campus are interfered with, the protective shroud of the First Amendment is removed.

It must be remembered that the court is the essential bastion of established order; it is the defender not only of the dissenter, but of those who wish to pursue their lawful activities peacefully. Thus once dissent exceeds the bounds of peaceful protest, the defense of libertarian motivation is irrelevant. In this sense the revolutionary is quite correct when he argues that the courts are the protectors of the "Establishment." The rules of the "Establishment," however, are in the last analysis the rules of society expressed in its laws. What every revolutionary is really saying then is that he has lost faith in achieving change through the existing procedures and is prepared to go outside society's rules to secure his ends. So be it; but in so doing he must recognize that at this point the law will regard him, rather than society or the university, as the oppressor, as the violator of the First Amendment. Exhortations to violence in a tense campus situation may very well be shouting "fire" in a crowded theatre.

[23]*Ibid.*

Scoggin v. Lincoln University
United States District Court, W.D. Missouri, 1968
291 F. Supp. 161.

JOHN W. OLIVER, District Judge:

Plaintiffs, two students of Lincoln University, a State supported institution, filed a complaint in which they alleged that defendants, the governing officials of that institution, acting under color of State law, deprived them of rights guaranteed them by the First, Fifth and Fourteenth Amendments to the Constitution of the United States. Jurisdiction was appropriately invoked under Section 1343(3) of Title 28, United States Code and Section 1983 of Title 42, United States Code. . . .

Findings of fact. The parties stipulated and agreed that:

On Wednesday, October 18, 1967, at approximately 5:30 p.m., a disturbance occurred during the supper hour in the cafeteria of the Lincoln University Student Union Building while a large number of students were gathered either eating or waiting to be served. The disturbance included the dropping of trays of food, the upturning of tables and chairs and the throwing of dishes and glassware. Approximately $1,500 damage was done to property of the University.

On October 19, 1967, the Committee on Student Personnel Services . . . convened for the purpose of investigating the occurrence and recommending disciplinary action where appropriate. . . .

On October 20, 1967, the Committee placed formal charges against the plaintiffs and other students for

planning and/or participating in a demonstration which led to destruction of University property on Wednesday, October 18, 1967, at the Student Union Building.

. . . On October 24, 1967, the Committee voted to recommend suspension of the plaintiffs for the remainder of the school year ending May 31, 1968. . . .

The problem of the cost and quality of the food served in the cafeteria at Lincoln University was not of recent origin. Demonstrations concerning that situation occurred at least as early as the year preceding the current incident. Exhibit J was a copy of a memorandum dated October 14, 1967, from Dean of Students Pugh to all

Lincoln University students on the subject of an increase in board costs that went into effect for the Fall semester in 1967. That notice, posted the Saturday before the disturbance occurred that following Wednesday, stated:

It has come to the attention of the Dean of Students that there is considerable concern, among a good number of our students, about the recent increase in the cost of a university room and board contract. This note is written with the hope that (1) some of your questions will be answered, and (2) that some light might be shed on a few areas of misunderstanding.

The Dean then set forth three reasons for the increase and concluded as follows:

There has been some talk of organized demonstrations to protest Cafeteria conditions; and it is understood that the movement toward such displays of dissatisfaction is already afoot.

It is hoped we can resolve said situation without a demonstration, through the efforts of our S.G.A. [Student Council], Catering Management representatives, and our "Cafeteria Board."

But if it becomes apparent that we "must" demonstrate, it is hoped we (1) respect the rights of those who may not share in our decided methods, (2) be orderly and peaceful, and (3) respect and care for university property.

. . . The single charge formulated against all seven students was that each was allegedly guilty of:

Planning and/or participating in a demonstration which led to the destruction of University property on Wednesday, October 18, 1967, at the Student Union Building.

Consideration of student activity and of the later proceedings before the discipline committee must be viewed in light of the notice given all students on October 14, 1967, which stated that "if it becomes apparent that we 'must' demonstrate [to protest Cafeteria conditions] it is hoped we (1) respect the rights of those who do not share in our decided methods, (2) be orderly and peaceful, and (3) respect and care for university property."

. . . Viewed as a whole, it is apparent that the committee proceeded on the unarticulated assumption that if the evidence established that a particular student, including both plaintiffs, had helped plan *any sort* of a demonstration they should be disciplined.

A large part of the difficulty concerning this case arose from indiscriminate use of the word "demonstration." We do not indulge in legal niceties when we factually recognize that the word "demonstration" means different things to different people on the campus today. Dean Pugh's public announcement of October 14, 1967, used that word in the sense that clearly contemplated that the anticipated student "demonstration" would be peaceful in nature and that appropriate respect would be accorded the rights and property of others. . . .

Evidence that related to students other than the plaintiffs, however, established that a few particular students at Lincoln University viewed a student "demonstration" as an occasion for violent confrontation with what they would label part of the Establishment. That essentially nihilistic notion rejects the fundamental idea of our democracy that the exercise of rights guaranteed by the Bill of Rights of the Constitution of the United States is an effective instrument for change. Indeed, that view accepts the related anarchical notion that a modern day student "demonstration" must, in order to be effective, include destruction, violence, and sometimes obscenity so that attention is focused on the asserted decadence and obsolescence of the institution under attack.

The Committee's charge that plaintiffs planned and participated in a "demonstration which led to the destruction of University property" must be read in light of the meaning given the word "demonstration" by the committee and must be considered as a charge that plaintiffs in fact planned a "demonstration" different in kind from that authorized and contemplated in Dean Pugh's October 14, 1967, notice or that plaintiffs had in fact personally participated in the destruction of University property.

Our review of the Committee's proceedings leaves us with a firm conviction that the Committee's consideration of the data before it rested on the premise that it was not necessary to establish that plaintiffs had either (a) planned a demonstration different from that contemplated by Dean Pugh's October 14, 1967, notice or (b) that they had personally destroyed University property.

So far as the two plaintiffs involved in this case are concerned, the proceedings of the Committee demonstrate that there was no substantial evidence to support a finding that those two students had in fact planned a demonstration different from that authorized on October 14, 1967, or that either had in fact personally destroyed University property.

Although counsel argue to the contrary, it is perfectly clear that the Committee was convinced that neither plaintiff actually destroyed any University property. Plaintiffs' names were omitted from the list of students finally named as "persons known to the Committee as involved actively . . . in destroying state or university property." Plaintiffs' names were in fact included on a separate list of persons whom the Committee believed had only "supported or helped plan or project the demonstration *which led to* the destruction of state or university property."

It is obvious that no student could properly be disciplined for planning, participating, or urging others to participate in the sort of "demonstration" contemplated by the October 14, 1967, notice.

Data that plaintiff Scoggin was in favor of a "demonstration" cannot, as counsel for defendants suggest, be considered as substantial evidence that he planned a demonstration different in kind from that authorized by the October 14, 1967, notice. Statements, for example, in the Committee's proceedings to the effect that "Mr. Scoggin was in student meetings openly advocating quick and definite action of the students in the matter of a demonstration on the campus, and refusing to accept any other solution to the alleged problems," without more, does not constitute substantial evidence that plaintiff Scoggin had in mind any different kind of demonstration than that anticipated by the October 14, 1967, notice. Such isolated statements in the Committee's proceedings must be read in context.

Plaintiffs were not charged with having incited other students to destroy property. There is no substantial evidence to support such a charge had it been made. Plaintiffs' suspension cannot be justified on the basis suggested by defendants.

We find and determine that the Committee's charge against plaintiffs did not appropriately distinguish between action that the plaintiffs could legally take and action for which the Committee could lawfully impose disciplinary sanctions. In hearing and considering the testimony of the witnesses and in making its recommendation of suspension we find that the Committee could not and did not properly differentiate between plaintiffs' right to plan and to participate in the sort of demonstration authorized by the October 14, 1967, notice and the Committee's unquestioned right to discipline students for unlawful conduct, including, but not in any way limited to, the planning and knowing participation in the sort of violent and destructive "demonstration" that occurred on October 18, 1967.

We further find that the Committee apparently determined that proof that the October 18, 1967, "demonstration" did in fact lead to the destruction of University property was sufficient substantial evidence that all persons, including plaintiffs, who played an active part in the planning of, or who participated in that "demonstration" must have known and intended that it would be a violent one, inconsistent with the sort of demonstration authorized by the October 14, 1967, notice.

On the basis of all the facts and circumstances we must and do find that the disciplinary action taken against plaintiffs was not based upon adequate substantial evidence to support its imposition. The defendants' suggested findings of fact are refused for the reasons stated. . . .

Siegel v. Regents of The University of California et al.

United States District Court, N.D. California, 1970
308 F. Supp. 832.

SWEIGERT, District Judge:

This suit is brought under the Civil Rights Act, 42 U.S.C. Sec. 1983, for injunctive and declaratory relief and for damages. . . .

The facts shown by the record are in substance and effect that plaintiff Siegel is a student enrolled at the School of Law on the Berkeley Campus of the University of California. On May 15, 1969, he was President-elect of the Associated Students, University of California, designated by the Chancellor of the Berkeley Campus as the student government organization at that campus.

As of May 15, 1969, certain real property belonging to defendant The Regents, and situated in the vicinity of the Berkeley Campus, had been forcibly seized and occupied by persons not acting under the control or direction of defendant Regents. On the morning of

May 15, 1969, The Regents caused a fence to be erected on the perimeter of said property.

On the same day a rally was held at the noon hour in Sproul Plaza on the Berkeley Campus. Several thousand persons were in attendance. Plaintiff Siegel addressed the rally and concluded his remarks as follows:

Now, we have not yet decided exactly what we are going to do. But there is some plans. I have a suggestion, let's go down to the Peoples Park, because we are the people. But a couple of things, a couple of points I would like to make. If we are to win this thing, it is because we are making it more costly for the University to put up its fence than it is for them to take down their fence. What we have to do then is maximize the cost to them, minimize the cost to us. So what that means, is people be careful. Don't let those pigs beat the shit out of you, don't let yourselves get arrested on felonies, *go down there and take the park* [emphasis added]. . . .

Immediately thereafter, several thousand persons proceeded from the rally down Telegraph Avenue toward the aforementioned property where they were met by law enforcement officers. Violence ensued resulting in the next few days in one death, numerous injuries and many arrests.

By letter dated May 20, 1969, defendant Shotwell, Coordinator of Facilities and Regulations, advised plaintiff in writing . . . that he was charged with violating certain specified regulations, copies of which were enclosed, by reason of his actions on May 15, 1969, in urging his audience to "go down there and take the park."

Plaintiff was also advised that a hearing had been set before the Berkeley Campus Committee on Student Conduct. . . .

The Committee on Student Conduct found and concluded:

. . . that the action of Mr. Siegel did constitute violations of the University's regulations on the Standard of Conduct by exposing the University and its people to mob formation and its attendant potential consequence of violence. Therefore the Committee as a whole agrees that disciplinary action is warranted. . . .

A majority of the Committee also concluded that Siegel:

. . . knowingly spoke at a rally in reckless disregard of the tense and angry nature of the crowd without regard to the foreseeable consequences. At best, his conduct exhibits inexcusable ignorance of the dangerous circumstances. . . .

The Committee recommended that the Chancellor approve the placing of Siegel on disciplinary probation, including exclusion from participation in all privileges or extracurricular activities and specifically from serving as President of the student government.

By letter dated July 2, 1969, . . . defendant Williams advised plaintiff of the Chancellor's acceptance of the recommendations of the Committee on Student Conduct and informed Siegel that he was placed on probation for a one-year period, the terms of probation permitting plaintiff the privileges of a student and privileges incidental to his studies, but prohibiting him from holding student government office or engaging in other extracurricular activities.

The preliminary injunction sought by plaintiff would enjoin defendants from imposing any discipline on plaintiff for his speech of May 15, 1969, and would require defendants to restore plaintiff forthwith to full student status with all rights and privileges thereof, including the right to hold and occupy the office of President of the Associated Students.

Plaintiff contends that the University regulations promulgated by the University, an agency of the State of California, are constitutionally invalid in that they are "overbroad" and "vague" restrictions upon the right of free speech protected by the First Amendment.

Upon this ground, plaintiff moves for the convening of a three judge court under 28 U.S.C. Sections 2281 and 2284.

Since the requirement for a three judge court is not applicable unless the court determines that the constitutional issues are substantial, we must first examine the record to make a determination of substantiality.

The regulations under which plaintiff was disciplined and which are attacked upon constitutional grounds by plaintiff, are as follows:

Section II, Part A, Standard of Conduct, provides that a student enrolling in the University assumes an obligation to conduct himself in a manner compatible with the University's functions as an educational institution, and that misconduct for which students are subject to discipline falls into the following categories:

Paragraph 3 prohibits obstruction or disruption of administration or other University activities, including its public service functions, or of other authorized activities on University premises.

Paragraph 4 prohibits physical abuse of any person on University owned or controlled property or conduct which threatens or endangers the health or safety of any such person.

Paragraph 7 refers generally to violation of University policies or of campus regulations concerning the use of University facilities. . . .

Paragraph 10 prohibits disorderly conduct on University owned or controlled property.

Paragraph 12 prohibits conduct which adversely affects the student's suitability as a member of the academic community. . . .

Substantiality of constitutional contentions. Although First Amendment rights of expression, applied in the light of the special characteristics of school environment, are available to teachers and students (who, of course, do not shed their constitutional rights to freedom of speech or expression at the schoolhouse gate), school officials, nevertheless, have comprehensive authority to prescribe and control, consistently with constitutional safeguards, conduct which intrudes upon the work of the school. . . .

It is well settled that even speech or expression, which materially and substantially intrudes upon the work of the school by interfering with the requirements of appropriate discipline in its operation, may be prohibited. . . .

Regulations for these purposes, which reasonably set forth what conduct is expected from students, are sufficient and need not be tested by the strict standards applicable to criminal statutes or proceedings. . . .

It will be noted that the regulations in question here are on their face directed, not to speech or mere expression of opinion, but to conduct.

There is nothing in these regulations that could be fairly said to have a "chilling effect" upon a student's exercise of First Amendment rights of free speech or expression because of "vagueness" or "overbreadth" or otherwise.

Nor is the record such as to show that the regulations have been applied with that effect as to this particular plaintiff.

The complaint, itself, sets forth the exhortation by plaintiff at the close of his speech to "Go down and take the park" and the circumstances under which those words were uttered. . . .

Although the complaint alleges that this exhortation by plaintiff was intended by him as mere rhetoric and not for the purpose of directing a physical seizure of the park the complaint, nevertheless, discloses that plaintiff, President-elect of the Associated Students addressing 2,000 students already aroused over the park situation, told them to "Go down and take the park."

The record also shows that plaintiff has admitted by his own testimony at the hearing . . . that he attempted to make his comments sound militant so he wouldn't be tuned off; that he couldn't say simply "Now stay away from the police" because they would have told him to sit down; that he couldn't say it in those words because a moderate sounding statement "wouldn't have any effect on them, whereas a statement made in their own language would have a modifying effect on them, I hoped."

Under the circumstances shown by the record that statement transcends mere expression of opinion and becomes *conduct*—a distinct, affirmative *verbal act*—overt conduct for which plaintiff could be properly called to account under the regulations whatever might be his claim as to his subjective purpose and intent.

Illegal conduct is not protected merely because it is in part initiated, evidenced or carried out by language. Utterance in a context of violence, involving a clear and present danger, can lose its significance as an appeal to reason and become part of an instrument of force and as such unprotected by the Constitution. . . .

Obviously, such conduct, according to any reasonable, educational standard, would materially and substantially intrude upon University administration. . . .

Plaintiff also relies in great part upon *Soglin v. Kauffman*, 295 F. Supp. 978 (W.D. Wis. 1968). . . . In *Soglin* certain students were charged generally with "misconduct" (not based in any particular regulation) for having physically and intentionally blocked ingress and egress at a University building to prevent certain interviews being held in the building and, further, were charged with having in this way violated a particular University regulation allowing assembly and speech only by lawful means which would not disrupt University operations.

The court expressed the view that the general charge of "misconduct" was insufficient to support the disciplinary proceedings but, nevertheless (p. 996), refused to grant injunctive relief on that ground, stating that to do so "[would] leave the University defenseless, so far as its regulation of *conduct* is concerned would be to permit, and possibly to encourage, a situation in which many values, including the exercise of First Amendment freedoms themselves, might be impaired."

As to the specific speech regulation in question, which is distinguishable from the regulations here in question, the court held that, construed as a prohibitive regulation, it was vague and overbroad as a regulation of expression and enjoined its enforcement.

Plaintiff also cites *Scoggin v. Lincoln Univ.*, 291 F. Supp. 161 (N.D. Mo. 1968) as similar to the pending case. In *Scoggin* the court merely held that the students, charged with planning an unauthorized demonstration in the University cafeteria and suspended from the University, had not been accorded even minimal procedural due process in the disciplinary proceedings taken against them. The court did not hold that the regulation in question was either vague or overbroad, or that the University lacked power to discipline for the alleged conduct in question. On the contrary, the court recognized (p. 172) that student conduct "violative of a valid rule or regulation of an educational institution does not gain the protection of the First Amendment merely because such conduct is in part initiated, evidenced, or carried out by means of language, either spoken, written or printed."

The court concludes that the constitutional issues raised by plaintiff concerning the regulations in question are insubstantial. . . .

7

SANCTIONS OF
THE INSTITUTION

With the decline of the *in loco parentis* doctrine, there has been a corresponding expansion of the view that misconduct by a student outside the university campus, unconnected with any institutional function and not posing a threat to the welfare of the college or its students, is not subject to institutional discipline. These activities are considered unrelated to the educational function and are left to the ordinary civil authorities for action. With increasing frequency, however, universities have been faced with alleged disruptive activities occurring on the campus, if not in campus buildings. Such activities may not only constitute violations of the criminal code of the state but may also be violative of the rules and regulations of the college or university. In such a case the student may be subjected to sanctions by the criminal courts as well as by the educational institution. It has been argued that such dual sanctions constitute double jeopardy. For instance, a student entering and causing damage to a university building may be suspended or otherwise disciplined by the institution, and may also be arrested, tried, fined, and imprisoned by law enforcement agencies. He may further be subject to a civil suit for damages. Superficially, such a situation would indicate multiple punishment for a single act. Double jeopardy relates only to the criminal law, however, i.e., a person may not be tried twice for the same act. University sanctions are more closely analogous to administrative proceedings than to criminal trials, and the doctrine does not apply. Just as a liquor permittee may lose his license as well as be arrested for brawling in his place of business, so may the student be expelled from college and arraigned before a court for a single act. It is clearly proper, however, for each forum to note the penalty imposed by the other when considering the severity of the sanction. Similarly, when considering what course to pursue, the experienced administrator will not regard his alternatives as mutually exclusive, but will seek instead a combination that will best meet a particular circumstance. In general, the remedies available to an educational institution for disruptive activities are internal disciplinary procedures, resort to regular law enforcement agencies, and the use of the injunction.

INTERNAL REMEDIES

The first step for an educational institution is the pursuit of its own internal remedies for breaches of campus discipline. For years the conduct of an institution of higher education has been based upon the assumption that all members of the university community will adopt good faith adherence to a common code of conduct. Working on this assumption, various disciplinary codes have been adopted to ensure fair treatment for violations. As will be pointed out, recent court decisions, beginning with the *Dixon* case,[1] have established the principle that the due process provisions of notice and hearing should apply to these matters. Clearly, from the institution's point of view, it would be best if cases of campus misconduct, other than obvious breaches of the criminal law, could be handled in this manner. Cases of the latter type or of disturbances of a continuous nature are often not susceptible to this treatment, however. For instance, continued disruption of university functions by nonstudents or by students who are prepared to sacrifice their status in the academy, clearly cannot be managed by institutional sanctions. The workings of a university's internal disciplinary system depend in the last analysis on its good

[1]*Dixon v. Alabama*, 186 F. Supp. 945 (1960) (M.D. Ala.).

faith acceptance by all members of the community. When this acceptance breaks down or when events are so severe as to be beyond its scope, recourse must be had to other remedies.

CRIMINAL LAW

The university may properly invoke the aid of legal law enforcement agencies for actions occurring on the campus. The prudent administrator, however, seeks to exhaust all possible remedies by use of his most important tool—persuasion. Indeed, it has become an article of conventional wisdom among educators that the police are called on the campus only as a last resort. To avoid the often unfortunate police-student confrontation, the sanctions of the criminal law are used in other ways. Increasingly, institutions faced with disruptive action will employ photographers, scanning cameras, television clips, and other devices, as well as plain clothes police and other individuals who will mix with the crowd and identify potential law breakers. This evidence is then turned over to the law enforcement authorities, who, after making identifications and securing statements, will swear out warrants. It should be noted that once the police are called on the campus or this material is made available to them, the decision to arrest and prosecute moves from the institution to the law enforcement agency. Indeed, some police departments may require that college presidents sign a statement that they will remain aloof from any prosecutions as a condition to the police entering the campus.

Experience has shown that exclusive reliance upon the regular law enforcement agencies may often result in wholesale arrests and trials. This leads to clogged court dockets and interminable delays. The delays are further compounded by the galaxy of procedural defenses available to any accused in our criminal courts. An experienced criminal lawyer will often require a space of several months to a year on a normal docket to present a proper defense. Motions for more specific statements, suppression of evidence, change of venue, as well as painstaking jury selection, are perfectly legitimate measures designed to ensure a fair trial. Add to this an extensive appeal procedure and one may readily appreciate why the use of the regular law enforcement procedure has been ineffective in cooling off a disruptive situation. Since criminal procedures militate against prompt disposition and since calling in the police may result in a police-student confrontation that might only aggravate the existing crisis, some administrations have turned to use of the injunction as a device to quell campus unrest. In several respects the injunction has been found preferable, for it avoids immediate use of police, allows a cooling off period if obeyed, and, in the event of a violation, provides quick and flexible punishments.

INJUNCTION

The injunction is what is known in law as an "equitable" remedy. This term arises from the original distinction between courts of law and courts of equity. In the developmental period of common law, it was realized that in many circumstances the law did not provide an adequate remedy. For instance, if one contracted for the services of an artist and he subsequently refused to perform, how was the court to measure money damages? In an attempt to meet this problem, the so-called courts of equity were developed in England, presided over by the chancellor. These courts would hear prayers for relief, based upon a claim that no adequate remedy existed before the courts of law. With the passage of time, the courts of equity developed their own body of law to deal with recurring questions. The separation between the courts of law and equity continued into the nineteenth century, at which time they were merged into a single system. Thus, in the United States today there is no distinction between remedies at law and equity as far as the court structure goes. The traditional bases for equitable jurisdiction and injunctive relief have been the probability of irreparable injury, the inadequacy of money damages, and a desire to prevent a multiplicity of suits. Universities have successfully contended that the disruption of academic life, the loss of time by students and professors, and the destruction of files and research papers constitute irreparable injury for which money damages are inadequate.

When injunctive relief was first sought against student disruption, the defense submitted that equitable jurisdiction was improper, since criminal statutes existed under which students could be prosecuted and that applying injunctive relief would usurp the jurisdiction of the criminal process. Universities argued that the delays inevitably associated with proceedings in the criminal courts rendered that remedy inadequate. In addition, they pointed out that public nuisances, boycotts or other interference with business, the keeping of disorderly houses, and the disturbance of public worship have been enjoined by the courts even though alternative remedies were available through criminal process. Finally, the educational institutions argued that continuing acts of disturbance are in the nature of a continuing trespass, which a court of equity has always been ready to enjoin.

A legal encyclopedia states:

The courts draw a distinction between mere temporary trespasses and those of a continuing or recurring nature. For the former, the remedy at law is usually adequate and will preclude injunction, whereas the injury from repeated or continuing trespasses is generally irreparable, in the sense that money compensation recoverable in legal actions will not fully remedy the wrong done, and any attempt to obtain relief at law would not only entail considerable expense in proportion to the benefits received, but would necessitate a multiplicity of suits, which is both a grievance to the parties and a burden to the public. Accordingly, continuing and repeated trespasses will generally be restrained where, from the pleadings and the facts, the court is satisfied that the injury caused thereby is otherwise irreparable, particularly where such continuing and repeated trespasses are not only negligent, but also wilful.[2]

Since 1969 the courts have proven increasingly ready to adopt the universities' arguments and are prepared to issue injunctions against continued disruption on the campus.

Courts are loath to issue injunctions indiscriminately. When a demonstration is short and poses no threat of substantial disruption, a court may choose not to interfere lest it infringe on the First Amendment rights to speech and assembly. If there is an absence of actual violence, the demonstrators have an opportunity to show cause why an injunction should not be issued. If the demonstration consists of multiple trespasses and involves substantial disruption, an *ex parte* (without hearing) injunction may issue and all demonstrators who had had notice of the injunction and who may be shown to have violated its terms may be found guilty of contempt of court.

[2] 28 *American Jurisprudence* 645 (Rochester, N.Y.: The Lawyer's Cooperative Publishing Co., 1964).

It should be noted that the injunction is enforced not by the criminal courts, but by the court or judge issuing it. The essence of this sanction is that it is an order of the court prohibiting acts that have been deemed to threaten irreparable injury. The court itself will not generally police it. Rather, the injured parties are usually expected to ensure compliance. This procedure is particularly significant in a campus situation. Once a university has secured injunctive relief from the court, it is expected to inform the court of any violations and to seek imposition of appropriate sanctions. In this sense the injunction is analogous to calling in law enforcement officers; once either act is done, the university loses some of its flexibility. In the former case, the court rather than the university becomes the judge of whether its order has been violated, and also decides the appropriate penalty.

The technical method of enforcement of the injunction is for the aggrieved party to present a motion for contempt. Essentially, "contempt" is the neglect or refusal to obey an order of the court, and an immediate hearing may be had without a jury and without the elaborate procedural requirements of the criminal law. The penalties vary with each state, and usually include provisions for both fine and imprisonment. In the federal courts a contempt sentence of up to six months may be imposed without a jury.

A further element of this remedy should be noted. An aggrieved person may request both temporary and permanent injunctions. It is the former that concerns us here. This is an order of the court used to maintain the status quo pending a hearing for permanent injunction, usually at least some weeks in the future. In the university context, the temporary order thus becomes an effective cooling off device. Its effect is magnified when one considers that the courts generally treat such orders as temporary only, and do not allow an appeal.[3] Theoretically, at least, a judge might incorporate unconstitutional restrictions in his order without fear of review by a higher court. The argument has been made that temporary as well as permanent injunctions should be appealable, but the United States Supreme Court has declined to review the issue.[4] The unspoken

[3] *Olcott v. Pendleton*, 128 Conn. 292 (1941).
[4] *Roach v. Connecticut*, 395 U.S. 979 (1969), certiorari denied.

rationale may be that a defendant can have the order made permanent and thus reviewable in less time than it takes to perfect an appeal.

CONCLUSION

One of the fascinating aspects of law in the United States has been its responsiveness to the demands of a changing society. Although the cynic might charge that the Supreme Court follows the election returns, the lawyer would argue rather that the courts are sensitive to the need for a body of law that is flexible enough to accommodate change without disrupting the accomplishments of the past. It is submitted that this is precisely what has occurred in the case of campus disorder. It became obvious that internal discipline and the sanctions of the criminal law were unsatisfactory methods to meet the unique problem of widespread disruption on the campus. What was necessary was a remedy that combined effective deterence with speedy execution. The injunction proved to be such a device. Indeed, its very existence has provided important leverage once the full implications of its use were understood by administrators and students. One must recognize, however, that the temporary injunction, with its immediate contempt provisions, lack of jury trial, and unappealable nature, is susceptible to abuse. Its use should thus be sparing in circumstances in which the other alternatives of negotiation and internal discipline have proven fruitless. The courts themselves must be attentive to this problem so that an overdependence on swift action does not result in the feared chilling effect on free speech. In essence, the remedy should be utilized only when the danger is imminent and the damage irreparable.

Sample Injunction Papers

TO THE SHERIFF OF THE COUNTY
OF ——, OR HIS DEPUTY:
GREETING

BY AUTHORITY OF THE STATE OF —— You are hereby commanded to summon JOHN DOE AND JANE ROE of the Town of ——, County of ——, and others on the campus of the University of —— in ——, to appear before the Superior Court to be held at —— on the First Tuesday of January 1975 at 10:00 A.M. then and there to answer unto the STATE OF —— in a civil action wherein the Plaintiff complains and says:

1. The Plaintiff is a sovereign state of the United States of America.

2. Pursuant to Chapter 000 of the General Statutes, Revision 1958, the State of —— has created the University of —— and empowered its Board of Trustees to make rules for the governance of said University and determine its general policies. See Section 00-000 of the General Statutes.

3. Pursuant to said Chapter 000 of the General Statutes, the University of —— operates and maintains an institution of higher education in the Town of ——.

4. On December 25, 1974, the defendants and others did impair the lawful activities, processes and functions of the University of —— in ——, in that they:

    a. Unlawfully entered and remained on portions of the University grounds which had been prohibited to them;

    b. Unlawfully prevented ingress and egress to and from said grounds and University buildings for persons lawfully entitled to so use;

    c. Unlawfully assaulted individuals seeking to use said premises as aforesaid;

    d. Unlawfully refused to cease and desist from such unlawful activity when directed to do so by University officials;

    e. Unlawfully impeded the free flow of traffic on the roads and walkways of the University;

    f. Unlawfully threatened to continue such disruptive activities.

5. The Defendants' continued disruption of lawful University activities will greatly impede its functions and is otherwise illegal and contrary to the public policy of the State of ——.

6. Unless a temporary restraining order is issued, substantial and irreparable injury to the Complainant or its property will be unavoidable.

7. Said unlawful acts have been threatened and will be committed by the Defendants unless said Defendants are restrained therefrom; greater injury will be inflicted upon the Plaintiff by the denial of relief than would be inflicted upon the Defendants by the granting of relief; and the Plaintiff has no adequate remedy at law.

The Plaintiff claims:

1. A temporary restraining order, ex parte, restraining the Defendants from any act which might impair or prevent the accomplishment of any lawful activity, process or function of the University of ——, including the disruption of placement interviews and unlawful entry into or upon the land and buildings of the University of ——.

2. Temporary and permanent injunctions to the like effect.

3. Such other relief as in law and equity may have pertained.

Hereof fail not but of this Writ, with your doings thereon, make due return according to law.

Dated at —— this 1st day of January, 1975.

Ret. 1st Tuesday
January 1975

STATE OF ——	SUPERIOR COURT
v.	—— COUNTY
JOHN DOE, ET AL.	JANUARY 1, 1975

Order of Notice

Notice to: All persons on the grounds of the University of —— in the Town of ——, County of ——, and the State of ——.

Upon the complaint of the Plaintiff in the above entitled action praying, for reasons therein set forth, for a temporary restraining order, temporary and permanent injunctions, returnable to the Superior Court within and for the County of —— at —— on the first Tuesday of January 1975, and upon a motion in said action for an order of notice, it appearing to and being found by the subscribing authority that notice most likely to come to the attention of the above is that hereinafter ordered:

It is

ORDERED THAT, notice of the institution of said action be given said Defendants by some proper officer or indifferent person causing a true and attested copy of this order of notice, and of the temporary restraining order issued by this Court on January 1, 1975, to be posted upon the door of the building in which recruitment interviews are held or the buildings being illegally occupied or blocked by the Defendants, and also by causing the substance of said restraining order to be as widely disseminated as may be practicable by means of radio and television stations in the vicinity of ——.

Judge, Superior Court

Ret. 1st Tuesday
January 1975

STATE OF ——	SUPERIOR COURT
v.	—— COUNTY
JOHN DOE, ET AL.	JANUARY 1, 1975

Temporary Restraining Order

The complaint and application for a temporary restraining order, ex parte, temporary and permanent injunctions with supporting affidavit, as on file, having been presented to the undersigned, the Court makes the following finding of facts:

1. That unlawful acts have been threatened and will be committed unless the same are restrained;

2. That substantial and irreparable injury to the Complainant or its property will follow;

3. That after each item of relief granted, greater injury would be inflicted upon the Complainant by the denial of relief than would be inflicted upon the Defendants by the granting of relief;

4. That the Complainant has no adequate remedy at law;

5. That unless a temporary restraining order is issued without notice, substantial and irreparable injury to the Complainant or its property will be unavoidable.

It appearing to the undersigned authority that a temporary restraining order ought to be issued, without notice,

These are, therefore, by authority of the State of —— to command and enjoin John Doe, Jane Roe, and others on the campus of the University of ——, and each of you, under penalty of $1,000, to refrain from any act which might impair or prevent the accomplishment of any lawful activity, process or function of the University of ——, including the disruption of placement interviews and unlawful entry into or upon the land and buildings of the University of —— until a hearing on a temporary injunction has been determined on January 5, 1975, or until further order of the Court in the premises herein.

Said temporary restraining order shall apply also to all persons on the grounds of the University of —— in ——.

_____
Judge, Superior Court

Dated: January 1, 1975

8

THE FOURTEENTH AMENDMENT AND THE STUDENT— ACADEMIC DUE PROCESS

All persons born or naturalized in the United States, and subject to the jurisdiction thereof, are citizens of the United States and of the state wherein they reside. No state shall make or enforce any law which shall abridge the privileges or immunities of citizens of the United States; nor shall any state deprive any person of life, liberty, or property, without due process of law; nor deny to any person within its jurisdiction the equal protection of the laws.[1]

In June 1969, Earl Warren retired as Chief Justice of the United States. The role of the former Chief Justice and his Court in the continuing growth of American jurisprudence will be debated for decades. One of the principal points of controversy has been and will be the Court's almost continuous expansion of the Fourteenth Amendment in the field of criminal law. Often overlooked are several more subtle influences the Supreme Court's actions have had on other courts of law acting in other fields, including the due process rights of students vis-à-vis educational institutions.

Any discussion of due process invites confusion unless some distinction is drawn between its procedural and substantive aspects.

[1]U.S. Constitution, Amendment XIV, Section 1.

119

In terms of academic procedural due process, the basic question is what procedures for hearing and notice are legally required to ensure fairness in student discipline. Substantive due process emphasizes not methods, but basic reasons and motives, e.g., what constitutes proper cause of dismissal.

PROCEDURAL DUE PROCESS—
THE REQUIREMENT OF A HEARING

Volume 14 of *Corpus Juris Secundum*, a standard legal encyclopedia, contains the title, Colleges and Universities. Section 26 thereof is headed *Government and Discipline* and contains the following statement:

The courts have upheld the validity of a regulation reserving to the university the right to dismiss a student at any time for any reason without divulging its reason. The general purpose of the regulation being recited has been to safeguard ideals of scholarship and moral atmosphere. . . .

The Federal District Court in Alabama agreed in 1960 in the case of *Dixon v. Alabama*, stating: "The prevailing law does not require the presentation of formal charges or a hearing prior to expulsion by the school authorities. . . ."[2] On appeal, the Court of Appeals for the Fifth Circuit disagreed. "Whenever a governmental body acts so as to injure an individual, the Constitution requires that the act be consonant with due process of law."[3] For this purpose, a state educational system is considered a governmental body.

Something obviously happened to judicial thinking during the course of the *Dixon* litigation. This something was a recognition by the court that state-supported educational institutions, as well as judicial, legislative, and administrative bodies, are subject to the constitutional requirements of the Fourteenth Amendment. The extension of concepts of due process to the educational scene is worth reviewing in some detail.

The Good Old Days. The earliest views of education in America regarded attendance at a college or university, be it public or private, as a privilege that could be denied or revoked by the institution.[4]

---

[2]186 F. Supp. 945, 952 (1960) (M.D. Ala.).

[3]*Dixon v. Alabama State Board of Education,* 294 F.2d 150 (1961) (5th Cir.); certiorari denied, 368 U.S. 930 (1961).

[4]*Board of Trustees v. Waugh,* 105 Miss. 623, 62 So. 827 (1913).

Being a privilege, the due process provisions of the Constitution of the United States were not applicable, and dismissal could occur largely at the discretion of the institution. The rationale for permitting such a wide exercise of discretion was a recognition by the court that the relationship between the student and the institution was something very special. In effect, the courts felt that an educational institution alone possessed the necessary expertise and sensitivity to prescribe rules and regulations necessary to promote and preserve the proper atmosphere for learning. It was accepted that the university must have the authority to act quickly for the rest of the student body. As Thomas Jefferson remarked, after the University of Virginia moved swiftly to dismiss students involved in a disorder:

It determined the well-disposed among them to frown upon everything of the kind hereafter, and the ill-disposed returned to order from fear, if not from better motives. A perfect subordination has succeeded, entire respect towards the professors, and industry, order and quiet, the most exemplary, has prevailed ever since.[5]

Jefferson's thinking was employed not only in educational circles but also by the courts. In addition, the judiciary developed a variety of theories that were utilized to verbalize in legal phraseology the peculiar status of the student before the law.

The earliest theory utilized for this purpose is the so-called doctrine of *in loco parentis*. This useful fiction cast the university in the role of a parent-substitute, literally "in place of parents." As such, the university-parents had a wide discretion to formulate rules of conduct as well as to punish their infraction. The natural corollary of this approach was, of course, that the student-child owed the institution-parent the corellative duty of prompt and unquestioning obedience.[6]

The extent to which this idyllic legal relationship was mirrored in fact may be questioned. In any event, few institutions today would presume to claim such authority (or responsibility). Instead, a college's assertion of wide discretionary authority is far more likely to be based upon an alleged express or implied contract between the university and the student. The basis of this contract theory is a promise

[5]18 *Writings of Thomas Jefferson* 348 (1904).
[6]*Gott v. Berea,* 156 Ky. 376, 161 S.W. 204 (1913); *John G. Stetson University v. Hunt,* 88 Fla. 510, 102 So. 637 (1924).

by the entering student to abide by the institution's rules and regulations, particularly those set forth in the catalog. These latter provisions characteristically contain a broad reservation to the college of authority to dismiss, suspend, or otherwise discipline without hearing for "conduct unbecoming," "insubordination," "appropriate reason," and the like. The results of such a theory are predictable. In New York, a court upheld the summary dismissal of a senior female student from Syracuse University on the grounds that she was not ". . . a typical Syracuse girl."[7] In that case, the catalog stated that ". . . the University reserves the right to require the withdrawal of any student at any time for any reason deemed sufficient to it, and no reason for requiring such withdrawal need be given."[8]

The contract analysis utilized by the courts has been criticized as being inappropriate because of the unequal bargaining position of the parties as well as questionable consideration.[9] Although most authorities have concurred in these reservations, the theory still is revived on occasion by certain courts, especially when private institutions are involved.[10]

In summary, then, the main body of law prior to the present decade recognized the right of the university to dismiss students summarily without hearing on any grounds it deemed sufficient. The only question on an appeal to the courts was whether the institution acted without malice and in accordance with its rules.

The maintenance of discipline, the upkeep of the necessary tone and standards of behavior in a body of students in a college is, of course, a task committed to its faculty and officers; not to the courts. It is a task which demands special experience, and is often one of much delicacy . . .; and the officers must, of necessity, be left untrammeled in handling the problems which arise as their judgment and discretion may dictate, looking to the ends to be accomplished. Only in extraordinary situations can a court of law ever be called upon to step in between students and the officers in charge of them.[11]

[7]*Anthony v. Syracuse University,* 223 N.Y.S. 796 (Sup. Ct. 1927), reversed 231 N.Y.S. 435 (App. Div. 1928).

[8]See Annot., 58 A.L.R. 2d 903, 905 (1958).

[9]3 *College Counsel* 16.

[10]*Carr v. St. John's University,* 34 Misc. 2d 319, 231 N.Y.S. 2d 403 (Sup. Ct. 1962).

[11]*Woods v. Simpson,* 146 Md. 547, 126 A. 882, 883 (1924).

The *Dixon* case has shattered this traditional approach.

The Dixon Case. In 1960, a group of black students at an Alabama state college engaged in a sit-in at a luncheon grill located in the basement of the Montgomery County Courthouse. The students were summarily expelled for this and other protests over segregated facilities in Alabama. The students replied by seeking an injunction in the Federal District Court against the State Board of Education and officials of the college. The main thrust of the petitioners' case was that, by expelling them without notice or hearing, the defendants had deprived them of rights guaranteed by the due process clause of the Fourteenth Amendment. The United States District Court did not agree. In a decision dated August 26, 1960, the court reflected the established approach to educational questions. It pointed out that the regulations of the College provided for expulsion for "conduct prejudicial to the school and for conduct unbecoming a student or future teacher in schools of Alabama, [or] . . . for insubordination. . . ."[12] In the Court's opinion, the right to attend the College was conditional upon compliance with its rules. The information in the hands of the College officials clearly substantiated a finding of insubordination, and no formal presentation of charges or a hearing was necessary.

The petitioners appealed to the Court of Appeals for the Fifth Circuit, and, on August 4, 1961, that tribunal reversed the District Court in a decision that has placed the state-supported educational bureaucracy firmly in the mainstream of modern due process standards. The Court, in effect, viewed the educational authority as analogous to an administrative agency, and stated that "whenever a governmental body acts so as to injure an individual, the Constitution requires that the act be consonant with due process of law."[13]

The *Dixon* case is fully in line with the other judgments of the Warren Court extending the protections of the due process clause of the Constitution to new areas of personal freedom. Understandably, the usual preoccupation is with affording due process to defendants in criminal proceedings. This emphasis should not lead to a neglect of the significance of due process in other fields, however. The history of the changing status of the student provides a compelling example

[12]*Dixon v. Alabama State Board of Education*, 186 F. Supp. 952.

[13]*Dixon v. Alabama State Board of Education*, 294 F.2d 155.

of legal development and growth in such a field. In fact, in the space of less than a decade, the principles enunciated in the *Dixon* case have become an accepted body of law. Any lingering doubts regarding this trend were dispelled by the United States District Court for the Western District of Missouri in a case involving the dismissal of three students from Central Missouri State College. One of the suspended students was named Esteban, and his claim of a denial of due process by the College was litigated in three separate judicial decisions entitled *Esteban v. Central Missouri State College*.[14] The final opinion in the *Esteban* case was written by Mr. Justice Blackmun, then sitting on the Court of Appeals for the Eighth Circuit. The litigation began with the appeal of the three student discipline cases to the Federal District Court for the Western District of Missouri. The judges of the Court recognized that the law on the subject was in a state of flux and accordingly, on its own motion, instituted a hearing before the full court. Briefs and oral arguments were invited from institutional, faculty, and student representatives, the American Civil Liberties Union, and the Attorney General of Missouri. The final order of the Court was unanimous and established judicial standards governing review of student discipline in tax-supported institutions. This court decision may very well be the model for the future and is worth examining in some detail.[15]

The court initially reviewed the lawful missions of tax-supported higher education and found that they included not only teaching, but also social criticism, commercial and industrial training, research, etc. This wide galaxy of functions was found not only lawful, but laudable, and students had the obligation to conduct themselves so as not to ". . . . intentionally act to impair or prevent the accomplishment of any lawful mission, process, or function of an educational institution."[16]

The Court stated clearly that if a student violated this standard, he subjected himself to institutional discipline. The court was unwilling to impose on college disciplinary proceedings the standards required in a criminal case, however.

[14]277 F. Supp. 649 (1967); 290 F. Supp. 622 (1968); 415 F.2d 1077 (1969).

[15]General Order on Judicial Standards of Procedure and Substance in Review of Student Discipline in Tax Supported Institutions of Higher Education, 45 F.R.D. 133 (1968) (W.D. Mo.) (U.S. Dist. Ct. for W.D. Mo., en banc).

[16]*Ibid.*, at 141.

The attempted analogy of student discipline to criminal proceedings against adults and juveniles is not sound. . . . The nature and procedures of the disciplinary process in such cases should not be required to conform to federal processes of criminal law.[17]

It was the opinion of this court that the federal court should not intervene unless there was a deprivation of due process, invidious discrimination, denial of federal rights, or clearly unreasonable, arbitrary, or capricious action.

Of most significance is the court's reference to due process. Expanding its remarks on this issue, the court stated that "in severe cases of student discipline . . . the institution is obligated to give to the student minimal procedural requirements of due process of law," citing the *Dixon* case.[18] The court then went further and set forth in outline form what these minimal requirements are.

First, the student should be given adequate notice in writing of the specific ground or grounds and the nature of the evidence on which the disciplinary proceedings are based. Second, the student should be given an opportunity for a hearing in which the disciplinary authority provides a fair opportunity for hearing of the student's position, explanations, and evidence. The third requirement is that no disciplinary action shall be taken on grounds which are not supported by any substantial evidence. Within limits of due process institutions must be free to devise various types of disciplinary procedures relevant to their lawful missions, consistent with their varying processes and functions and not an unreasonable strain on their resources and personnel.

There is no general requirement that procedural due process in student disciplinary cases provides for legal representation, a public hearing, confrontation and cross-examination of witnesses, warnings about privileges, self-incrimination, application of principles of former or double jeopardy, compulsory production of witnesses, or any of the remaining features of federal criminal jurisprudence. Rare and exceptional circumstances, however, may require provision of one or more of these features in a particular case to guarantee the fundamental concepts of fair play.[19]

In its decisions on the *Esteban* case itself, the court reiterated the *Dixon* rule that the Fourteenth Amendment applies to disciplinary procedures at a tax-supported university. It emphasized, however,

[17]*Ibid.*, at 142.
[18]*Ibid.*, at 147.
[19]*Ibid.*

that the proceedings need not be a formal court type judicial hearing such as is required in criminal cases.[20] Essentially, the due process requirement is one of notice, fair hearing, and a decision based upon the evidence. Judge Blackmun's decision of appeal reaffirmed these principles as well as those of the *Dixon* case. He stated:

> . . . it is not sound to draw an analogy between student discipline and criminal procedure. . . . school regulations are not to be measured by the standards which prevail for the criminal law and for criminal procedure; . . . After all, the test, we feel, is that of reasonableness.[21]

The foregoing remarks of the Court can well be interpreted as a caveat to every educational administrator that the time is now long past when disciplinary sanctions can be invoked without careful attention to the constitutional requirements of the Fourteenth Amendment. Indeed, the words of the Court can serve as the logical starting point for any state-supported institution seeking to devise appropriate procedures that not only provide for speedy discipline but also ensure protection of the basic rights of individuals.

PROCEDURAL DUE PROCESS
AND THE PRIVATE INSTITUTION

Although the courts have been flexible in extending the procedural protections of the Fourteenth Amendment to students of state-supported institutions, they have been reluctant to utilize a similar approach when dealing with private colleges and universities. The distinction goes back to *Dartmouth College v. Woodward*,[22] decided in 1816. In that case, the United States Supreme Court rejected the argument that Dartmouth was a state institution because it was incorporated by the state and dedicated to education.

Recently the question has been raised whether the principles of the *Dartmouth College* case apply to the modern university, which often derives a large proportion of its support from federal or state

---

[20]*Esteban v. Central Missouri State College*, 290 F. Supp. 622, 628-29 (1968) (W.D. Mo.).

[21]*Esteban v. Central Missouri State College*, 415 F.2d 1077, 1088, 1090 (1969) (8th Cir.).

[22]*Dartmouth College v. Woodward*, 4 U.S. (4 Wheat.) 518 (1816).

funds. A federal district court in Louisiana met this issue squarely in a case involving Tulane University.

At the outset, one may question whether any school or college can ever be so private as to escape the reach of the Fourteenth Amendment—No one any longer doubts that education is a matter affected with the greatest public interest. And this is true whether it is offered by a public or a private institution—Clearly, the administrators of a private college are performing a public function.[23]

The finding of the district court was reversed on rehearing, with the court holding that state action or involvement in the affairs of the Tulane board was not so significant that it could be said that the actions of the board were the actions of the State of Louisiana. A similar result was reached in the case of *Grossner v. Trustees of Columbia University*,[24] in which the court stated that "receipt of money from the state is not, without a good deal more, enough to make the recipient an agency or instrumentality of the Government."[25] The court suggested that it was necessary to demonstrate a substantial or relevant connection between the state and the University. A similar finding was reached by Judge Friendly in a 1968 case involving Alfred University.[26]

At the present time, it would appear that the courts are reluctant to extend the protection of the Fourteenth Amendment to students attending private colleges and universities. In view of the current economic realities facing these institutions, however, increased levels of governmental support that might invite further review of this question are possible. It should be noted that even the court in the *Alfred* case hedged a bit and declined to comment on the applicability of the First and Fourteenth Amendments if the private institution were to adopt discriminatory admission policies.

[23]*Guillory v. Administrators of Tulane University*, 203 F. Supp. 855 (1962) (E.D. La.), reversed on rehearing, 212 F. Supp. 674 (1962) (E.D. La.).

[24]287 F. Supp. 535 (1968) (S.D.N.Y.).

[25]*Ibid.*, at 547-548.

[26]*Powe v. Miles*, 407 F.2d 73 (1968) (2nd Cir.). The court stated: "We perceive no basis for holding that the grant of scholarships and financing . . . imposes on the state a duty to see that Alfred's overall policies with regard to demonstrations and discipline conform to First and Fourteenth Amendment standards so that state inaction might constitute an object of attack." 407 F.2d, at 81.

SUBSTANTIVE DUE PROCESS

The protection of the Fourteenth Amendment has two dimensions, procedural and substantive. These concepts are usually intertwined and an analysis of one without considering the other results in a less than accurate picture of the development of the law. Such is the case with issues of student discipline. In the earlier cases to which reference has been made, the issue of summary dismissal was almost invariably linked with allegations of inadequate grounds for discipline, e.g., not being a "typical Syracuse girl."[27] Under the earlier view, however, neither claim could prevail unless bad faith or arbitrary judgment on the part of the administrators was shown. This doctrine, of course, was consistent with the contract analysis, which the courts found particularly useful for disposing of issues of substantive due process as well.

As with the analysis in procedure cases, the judiciary's stated reasons for its reluctance to interfere was a recognition that proper educational administration required the allowance of substantial discretion. Once again, the *Dixon* case stands as a landmark, marking a change in approach. Although the bulk of that case was devoted to the question of the necessity for a fair hearing, the Court also indicated that the individuals sought to be disciplined must receive a list of specific charges, not merely vague allegations of "misconduct" or the like. The judicial break with the past did not prove as clear as it did on the issue of procedure, however. This uncertainty is evident when one considers the case of *Carr v. St. John's University*,[28] in which the plaintiff, who was in his senior year at a private Roman Catholic institution, was married in a civil ceremony. The institution's catalog stated that "in conformity with the ideals of Christian education and conduct the University reserves the right to dismiss a student at any time on whatever grounds the University judges advisable."[29]

Although the lower court felt that a civil ceremony did not violate "Christian ideals," it also held that the regulations were ambiguous and uncertain in that they did not sufficiently inform those who were subject to them of what conduct would render them liable

[27]*Anthony v. Syracuse University, supra* note 7.
[28]*Supra* note 10.
[29]*Ibid.*, at 407.

to penalties; the court ordered the student reinstated. The Appellate Division reversed and sustained the dismissal on the grounds that the prohibition of a civil ceremony was implicit in the Roman Catholic commitment of this particular private university, and that students and authorities at the University should be held to knowledge that a civil ceremony would be antithetical to the requirements of Catholic education and conduct.[30]

The issue of substantive due process has been significantly refined in recent cases. The one receiving the most popular publicity was that arising from the filthy speech movement on the Berkeley campus. In the case of *Goldberg v. Regents of the University of California*,[31] the court upheld University discipline through a recognition of the inherent power of the University to discipline for conduct that obstructs the goals of the institution.

Thus, the University has the power to formulate and enforce rules of student conduct that are appropriate and necessary to the maintenance of order and propriety, considering the accepted norms of social behavior in the community where such rules are reasonably necessary to further the University's educational goals.[32]

The result was a flexible, if not wholly satisfactory, balancing of competing interests such as frequently occurs in free speech cases under the First Amentment. A similar result was reached in *Buttney v. Smiley*,[33] in which the court upheld dismissal after hearing for disruption of C.I.A. employment interviews at the University of Colorado. The court in *Buttney* presented a cogent summary of its thinking:

The right of the University administration to invoke its disciplinary powers in this instance need not be entirely bottomed on any published rule or regulation. . . . It is an inherent power that the school administration authorities have to maintain order on its campus and to afford students, school officials, employees and invited guests freedom of movement on the campus and the right of ingress and egress to the school's physical facilities. We agree with the students that the doctrine of *"In Loco Parentis"* is

[30]*Carr v. St. John's University*, 231 N.Y.S.2d 410 (1962) (App. Div.).
[31]57 Cal. Rptr. 463 (1967) (C.A.).
[32]*Ibid.*, at 472.
[33]281 F. Supp. 280 (1968) (D. Colo.).

no longer tenable in a Univeristy community; and we believe that there is a trend to reject the authority of the University to regulate "off-campus" activity of students. However, that is not to say that conduct disruptive of good order on the campus should not properly lead to disciplinary actions.[34]

The foregoing case seems to indicate that issues of substantive due process gave way to concepts of implied or inherent powers on matters of student discipline, i.e., that obviously disruptive activity need not be specifically proscribed. Obviously any doctrine of implied or inherent powers can be utilized by an institution to cover a wide variety of situations not provided for by specific regulations. Nevertheless, the language in these cases must be read with a caveat arising from the 1968 disturbances at the University of Wisconsin. The Wisconsin case raises the issue of specificity, which has occupied the attention of criminal law observers for some time. Simply stated, the principle is that rules for conduct must be drawn with sufficient specificity that a reasonable person is appraised of just what conduct is prohibited. If a criminal statute does not meet this standard, it will be declared void for vagueness. Although the Colorado and California courts did not appear concerned with this doctrine for student cases, Judge Doyle in Wisconsin took the question very seriously.

In the case of *Soglin v. Kauffman*,[35] the plaintiff students brought an action for a declaratory judgment and an injunction seeking relief from prospective disciplinary action by the University for disruption of job interviews. The University had charged them with a variety of very specific acts of disruption, which it alleged constituted "misconduct" punishable by expulsion. Judge Doyle, in a rather ambiguous decision, expressed dissatisfaction with the use of such terms as "disrupt the operations of the University" or "misconduct" as standards of student conduct. In the judge's opinion, phrases such as these do not

contain even the most general description of the kinds of conduct which might be considered disruptive of the operations of the University, nor . . . undertake to draw any distinctions whatever as among various categories of university "operations."[36]

[34]*Ibid.*, at 286.
[35]295 F. Supp. 978 (1968) (W.D. Wisc.).
[36]*Ibid.*, at 993.

One has difficulty reconciling the approaches of the federal court in the California and Colorado cases, on the one hand, with the Wisconsin case on the other. The Federal Court for the Western District of Missouri apparently recognized this lack of certitude in the law when it determined to entertain its proceedings on this very issue. The Missouri court's remarks are as significant in the area of substantive due process as they are in the procedural area. In its order the court stated that an educational institution may establish

any standards reasonably relevant to the lawful missions, processes, and functions of the institution.[37]

In addition,

standards so established may apply to student behavior on and off the campus when relevant to any lawful mission, process, or function of the institution . . . and may require superior ethical and moral behavior.[38]

The court goes further.

If a duly promulgated standard is challenged, the institution must demonstrate that the standard is recognized as relevant to a lawful mission of the institution, and is recognized as reasonable by some reputable authority or school of thought in the field of higher education.[39]

The court recognized that detailed prohibitive codes can often be provocative, and suggested that general statements of affirmative standards of expected conduct might be a useful substitute. In what appears to be a rejection of Judge Doyle's approach, the court states that:

the legal doctrine that a prohibitory statute is void if it is overly broad or unconstitutionally vague does not, in the absence of exceptional circumstances, apply to standards of student conduct.[40]

CONCLUSION

There is no question that judicial thought on the status of students has been influenced by the view of the United States Supreme Court

[37]*Esteban v. Central Missouri State College*, 45 F.R.D. 133, 145 (1968) (W.D. Mo.).
[38]*Ibid*
[39]*Ibid.*, at 146.
[40]*Ibid.*

on questions of individual freedoms under the Fourteenth Amendment. Indeed, some suggest that the expanded concept of academic due process is in no small measure a reflection of the influence of the Warren Court. Whether this trend will continue is, of course, unpredictable. It is clear, however, that the image of the academy as a semi-autonomous haven has been shaken, especially as to the standards it may employ in its disciplinary codes and procedures.

The university community has been regarded by many as a self-governing association of scholars dedicated to teaching, intellectual inquiry, and the expansion of human knowledge. This special position rested in turn on certain implied assumptions, including a recognized consensus within the community itself as to proper conduct and procedures as applied to faculty, students, and administration. One of the results of the events of the last few years has been a breakdown in this consensus. Students and faculty have questioned and tested the established procedures for dissent, as well as the legitimacy of university jurisdiction in many areas; administrators have acknowledged the university's inability to maintain order and have resorted to the aid of law enforcement officials and the courts. Increasingly, the university is losing its separate identity and is becoming a part of the larger society. Some lament this as a departure from historic purpose; others praise it as an effort to be in the vanguard of social action; all agree that the change has occurred. If the assumptions buttressing the university's special position are weakened, so also is its claim to special treatment before the law.

The picture is neither complete nor tidy. Many institutions have retained their traditional posture, and even within individual universities certain schools, colleges, or departments function as they did a decade ago. These institutions do not present problems for judicial determination. The law directs itself to the dissenter, the questioner, and the nonconformist who challenge the established order. Just as the great majority of citizens never have personal contact with the practical workings of the criminal law, so most students do not concern themselves with the constitutionality of university disciplinary proceedings. For those who are involved, however, the questions are very real, especially if the proscribed activities have political overtones.

It is this political dimension that has prompted a new look at university discipline. A reading of the cases indicates that the type of litigated offense has become markedly different in the last ten years. Certainly not being a "typical Syracuse girl" or marrying outside the nominal faith of a religiously-oriented institution can have traumatic personal consequences; yet the courts felt that the matters were of personal or institutional rather than judicial concern. When one attempts to justify conduct by claims of constitutionally protected rights of free speech and assembly, however, a far more significant issue is presented. Undoubtedly, the educational institutions are better equipped than the courts to process routine disciplinary matters. This is especially true when discipline is viewed as a tool of effective counseling. Yet this may not be the case when the student's offense is in the vernacular of an extreme form of dissent. In such cases the courts will be more disposed to pay close attention to constitutionally posited arguments. It is submitted that this is the variable that distinguishes the more recent adjudications of the courts. Although one still observes a reluctance to enter the academic thicket, there is a growing trend toward requiring more specific codes of conduct and strict interpretation of the requirements of procedural due process.

These developments have significant ramifications for the administration of student discipline. This function has been traditionally handled as an administrative matter, usually by a dean of students or his staff. In recent years, this has been increasingly regarded as a manifestation of the traditional *in loco parentis* approach to student relations, and efforts have been made to include both students and faculty in the process. This trend should be regarded as salutory, especially in serious cases with political overtones, in which an administrative officer might find himself with divided loyalty. In such instances, the university might be well advised to ensure an impeccable tribunal by calling on some outside person to serve as a hearing officer. This official could be a member of the law faculty, a retired judge, or even an attorney experienced in constitutional issues. This is not to say that the university should completely abdicate its traditional role. Indeed, it would be anticipated that the best interests of both the student and the institution would be served by administrative handling of the great majority of discipline cases. For serious offenses with civil libertarian overtones, however, the university should develop imaginative mechanisms to ensure impartiality. If they don't, the courts may.

Soglin v. Kauffman
United States District Court, W.D. Wisconsin, 1968
295 F. Supp. 978.

JAMES E. DOYLE, District Judge:

This opinion deals with that branch of this action in which plaintiffs seek declaratory and injunctive relief with respect to Chapter 11.02 of the Laws and Regulations of the University of Wisconsin, and with respect to disciplinary proceedings based upon alleged "misconduct" rather than upon alleged violations of any express regulation or statute.

Plaintiffs are alleged to be ten students at the Madison campus of the University of Wisconsin, and an unincorporated association known as Students for a Democratic Society (Madison chapter). They undertake to sue on behalf of others similarly situated, as well as for themselves. Several of the defendants are alleged to be officials of the University of Wisconsin, having duties with respect to discipline. . . .

"Misconduct" as a Standard. The amended charges . . . allege rather specific behavior on the part of the named students and conclude with the following:

All of the foregoing constituting:
1. Misconduct, as well as
2. A violation of Chapter 11.02. . . .

If the term "misconduct," without more, may serve as a standard for disciplinary action, it is not essential to the defendants' position that Chapter 11.02 be vindicated as a prohibitory regulation. For reasons which will be explained herein, I turn initially to the broader contention of the defendants: that the term "misconduct" may serve as a standard for disciplinary action, and that no more specific or definite substantive rules are required as a prerequisite for disciplinary action.

With respect to the imposition of criminal sanctions in the non-university society, such a regime would grossly violate the Constitution of the United States. . . . A federal, state, or local statute, ordinance, regulation, order or rule, subjecting one to imprisonment or fine or other serious sanctions for "misconduct" would surely fall as unconstitutionally vague. Moreover, it would not be necessary that a challenger await the outcome of an attempted application of so vague a rule to him in a specific judicial or administrative proceeding, and then dispute the validity of the rule only as applied. He could challenge the prospective application of a vague rule and obtain a judicial declaration of its invalidity and injunctive relief against attempts to enforce it. . . .

Defendants here contend that, given the opportunity, they can prove that with respect to the events of October 18, those students who were subsequently subjected to disciplinary action had received prior warnings from certain university administrators that they would be punished if they performed the acts which they are alleged to have proceeded nevertheless to perform. It is not contended that defendants could prove that those administrators who issued the warnings were themselves (as distinguished, for example, from the board of regents or the faculty, Sec. 36.12, Wis. Stat.) empowered to promulgate generally applicable rules of conduct for university students. Nor could it be contended that the term "misconduct" itself prescribes intelligible standards or criteria by which these administrators might exercise discretion to issue a specific warning or order in a specific case. In the non-university society, in the absence of a reasonably clear rule or standard or criterion promulgated by those duly empowered to promulgate them, one may not be punished for violating the order of an administrator, such as a policeman. . . .

Moreover, the vagueness doctrine is not to be conceived as being limited solely to the concept of fair notice as an element of substantive due process. The vagueness doctrine embodies a First Amendment concept as well:

The objectionable quality of vagueness and overbreadth does not depend upon absence of fair notice to a criminally accused or upon unchanneled delegation of legislative powers, but upon the danger of tolerating, in the area of First Amendment freedoms, the existence of a penal statute susceptible of sweeping and improper application. *NAACP v. Button*, 371 U.S. 415, 432-433, 83 S.Ct. 328, 338, 9 L.Ed.2d 405 (1963). . . .

Whether a given rule "involves" First Amendment rights so as to require that it be looked to "more closely" is often relatively easy to determine: a rule against bank robbery does not; a rule regulating public gatherings probably does. A rule against "misconduct" is so grossly vague that possible involvement of First Amendment rights cannot be ignored. . . .

In exercising this power to discipline for misconduct, the university is not bound to promulgate any rules defining misconduct. The function of fair notice can be effectuated by means other than promulgation of rules of general application. For example, university administrators can inform particular students in advance of a particular occasion that if the students behave in a particular manner, they will be punished. Notice of this latter type is constitutionally sufficient with respect to university disciplinary matters, although the vagueness doctrine might render it invalid in certain non-university situations.

With respect to First Amendment guarantees as implemented both by the vagueness and overbreadth tests, it is sufficient that disciplinary action be reasonably related to the maintenance of that order and decorum necessary to performance of the university's function. This determination is to be made by the courts by balancing the governmental interest in the university's program against the individual student's interest in his freedom. This "balancing" test is sharply to be distinguished from the tests of vagueness and overbreadth ("facial invalidity"). Moreover, the balancing test is to be judicially applied prospectively, but case by case, after the disciplinary proceeding has been completed.

The reason for sparing disciplinary proceedings from the tests of vagueness and overbreadth, and particularly from prospective application of these tests, lies in the uniqueness of the university as an institution and in the university's historically demonstrated attachment to freedom.

Historically, universities and colleges and schools, both public and private, have enjoyed wide latitude in student discipline. Various "models" of the relationship between the university and its students have been employed by the courts for the purpose of determining the legal attributes of the relationship: parent-child (*in loco parentis*); owner-tenant; parties to a contract. Van Alstyne, "The Student as University Resident," 45 *Denver L.J.* 582-598 (1968). Whatever the model or combination of models employed, the dominant pattern has been judicial non-intervention in the discipline of students by faculty, administrators, school boards, trustees, or regents.

In recent years, however, courts have been increasingly disposed to intervene in school disciplinary situations involving major sanctions. This has been most marked when intervention has appeared necessary to assure that procedural due process is observed: for example, specification of charges, notice of hearing, and hearing. . . . But judicial intervention in school disciplinary cases in more recent years has not been confined to matters of procedural due process. The validity of substantive school rules has been the subject of judicial scrutiny. . . .

Underlying these developments in the relationship of academic institutions to the courts has been a profound shift in the nature of American schools and colleges and universities, and in the relationships between younger and older people. These changes seldom have been articulated in judicial decisions but they are increasingly reflected there. The facts of life have long since undermined the concepts, such as *in loco parentis*, which have been invoked historically for confering upon university authorities virtually limitless disciplinary discretion. . . .

The world is much with the modern state university. Some find this regrettable, mourning the passing of what is said to have been the old order. I do not share this view. But whether the developments are pleasing is irrelevant to the present issue. What is relevant is that the University of Wisconsin at Madison may continue to encompass functions and situations such as those which characterized a small liberal arts college of the early twentieth century (of which some no doubt exist today), but that it encompasses many more functions and situations which bear little or no resemblance to the "models" which appear to have underlain, and continue in some cases to underlie, judicial response to cases involving college or university discipline. What is relevant is that in today's world university disciplinary proceedings are likely to involve many forms of misconduct other than fraternity hazing or plagiarism, and that the sanctions imposed may involve consequences for a particular student more grave than those involved in some criminal court proceedings.

The question here concerns the relationship, in today's world, between the university board, faculty, and administrators as the governors, and students as the governed. Although there is considerable ferment in the universities about this very relationship, I see no constitutional bar to an arrangement by which the state vests in a board of regents and the faculty the power to govern a university and to discipline its students; nor do I see any constitutional bar to a prompt and severe disciplinary response to violence and rioting and other constitutionally unprotected conduct. The more precise question concerns the manner in which this power to govern and to discipline is exercised. It concerns whether the manner of its exercise is wholly immune to the application of the standards of vagueness and overbreadth. Even more precisely, it concerns whether the courts may—and if they may, whether they should—measure the sufficiency of university rules and regulations against these constitutional standards. . . .

Finally, then, the issue is reached whether admission to the University of Wisconsin as a student, and continued enrollment there, may be made to depend upon consent to a regime in which due process may be denied by vague prohibitory standards, or freedom of expression may be threatened or denied by vague or overly broad prohibitory standards. For the reasons I have discussed the answer must be no, unless there is some compelling reason why the university should escape this particular constitutional stricture, some reason why it should be wholly free to refrain from promulgating reasonably definite and narrow rules of conduct. In *Esteban v. Central Missouri State College*, 290 F. Supp. 622, 630 (W.D.Mo., W.D., 1968), it was said:

Judicial notice is taken that outstanding educational authorities in the field of higher education believe, on the basis of experience, that detailed codes of prohibited student conduct are provocative and should not be employed in higher education. See, Brady and Snoxell, *Student Personnel Work in Higher Education*, p. 378 (Houghton-Mifflin, Boston, 1961). For this reason, general affirmative statements of what is expected of a student may be preferable in higher education. Such affirmative statements should, of course, be reasonably construed and applied in individual cases.

I cannot agree that university students should be deprived of these significant constitutional protections on so slender a showing. The American Association of University Professors has declared:

Disciplinary proceedings should be instituted only for violation of standards of conduct defined in advance and published through such means as a student handbook or a generally available body of university regulations. Offenses should be as clearly defined as possible, and such vague phrases as "undesirable conduct" or "conduct injurious to the best interests of the institution" should be avoided. Conceptions of misconduct particular to the institution need a clear and explicit definition. Statement on The Academic Freedom of Students, 51 *A.A.U.P.Bull.* 447, 449 (1965). . . .

For the reasons stated, and upon the basis of the entire record herein, I conclude that the constitutional doctrines of vagueness and overbreadth are applicable, in some measure, to the standard or standards to be applied by the university in disciplining its students, and that a regime in which the term "misconduct" serves as the sole standard violates the due process clause of the Fourteenth Amendment by reason of its vagueness or, in the alternative, violates the First Amendment as embodied in the Fourteenth by reason of its vagueness and overbreadth.

I have said that these doctrines are applicable "in some measure." It is neither necessary nor wise presently to decide whether they are applicable to disciplinary proceedings in which the range of possible sanctions is mild, such as the denial of social privileges or a minor loss of academic credits or perhaps expulsion from a specific course or perhaps a brief suspension. Nor is it necessary or wise presently to decide whether the standards of vagueness and overbreadth are to be applied as stringently to university regulations of conduct as to criminal statutes in non-university life. Nor is it necessary or wise presently to decide whether these standards are to be applied with equal stringency in every phase of the life of the university; in non-university society, it appears that they are not applied with equal stringency to economic regulations, regulations of speech or assembly, public employment, penal institutions, court room decorum, the military establishment, and other situations; it may be that within the university community the standards may permissibly apply differently to the teacher's control of the classroom, demonstrations, dormitory life, picketing, parking regulations and decorum in disciplinary hearings.

The judgment here declared is that a standard of "misconduct," without more, may not serve as the sole foundation for the imposition of the sanction of expulsion, or the sanction of suspension for any significant time, throughout the entire range of student life in the university.

Chapter 11.02, Laws and Regulations of the University of Wisconsin. I turn, then, from the defendants' contention that the term "misconduct" alone is sufficient to support the imposition of serious disciplinary sanctions for the behavior which allegedly occurred on the campus on October 18. I turn to the only university rule or regulation, then in existence, which defendants continue to assert as a basis for such disciplinary sanctions. This is Chapter 11.02 of the Laws and Regulations of the Madison campus of the University of Wisconsin, which provides:

Scope of Student Freedom. Students have the right, accorded to all persons by the Constitution, to freedom of speech, peaceable assembly, petition and association. Students and student organizations may examine and discuss all questions of interest to them, and express opinions publicly as well as privately. They may support causes by lawful means which do not disrupt the operations of the University, or organizations accorded the use of University facilities.

. . . But in the view I have taken, expressed in the preceding section of this opinion, such vagueness or overbreadth, or both, are impermissible in the First Amendment area when the potential of serious disciplinary sanctions exists. When the standards of vagueness and overbreadth are applied to Chapter 11.02, however mildly, I am obliged to find it invalid. Neither the element of intention, nor that of proximity of cause and effect, nor that of substantiality, for example, is dealt with by its language. Nor does it contain even the most general description of the kinds of conduct which might be considered disruptive of the operations of the university, nor does it undertake to draw any distinctions whatever as among the various categories of university "operations."

I conclude that Chapter 11.02 is unconstitutionally vague.

Assuming, again with difficulty as was true with respect to "misconduct" as a standard, that the term "lawful means which do not disrupt the operations of the university" is sufficiently definite to avoid the vice of vagueness, I conclude that it is overly broad. As explained above . . . when the end can be more narrowly achieved, it is not permissible to sweep within the scope of a prohibition activities that are constitutionally protected free speech and assembly. And one may attack such an overly broad prohibition although his own conduct may have been constitutionally punishable had the rule been more narrowly drawn. . . .

To hold, as I have held herein, that the university may not escape the necessity to formulate reasonable definite and narrow regulations, at least in some areas of student life and at least with respect to the imposition of serious sanctions, will itself require a considerable readjustment within the university. To take a second step—that is, to confront the university with a sudden application of the tests of vagueness and of overbreadth in a prospective, anticipatory, and wholesale manner—is to impose too radical a transitional strain upon the institution. . . .

A reasonable time must be permitted for the university to review its situation. Even so, it will be necessary to compress into a very short interval a process which has required many years in non-university society. For the present, to grant injunctive relief and to leave the university defenseless, so far as its regulation of conduct is concerned, would be to permit, and possibly to encourage, a situation in which many values, including the exercise of First Amendment freedoms themselves, might be impaired.

I have concluded that injunctive relief with respect to the application of the standard of "misconduct," without more, should be denied in this action, and that the plaintiffs and the members of their classes should be left to seek judicial review of the validity of this standard retrospectively, case by case, as it has actually been applied. . . .

Sill v. Pennsylvania State University

United States District Court, M. D. Pennsylvania, 1970
318 F.Supp. 608.

NEALON, District Judge:

This action was instituted by twelve students at Pennsylvania State University (Penn State) against the Board of Trustees and the President of Penn State as a result of disciplinary action imposed on the students in June 1970, following a campus disturbance in April 1970. Declaratory and injunctive relief is sought to redress alleged violations of the students' rights under the First, Fifth and Fourteenth Amendments of the Constitution. . . .

Discussion. The law applicable to student's rights while attending a public school has developed rapidly in recent years and certain controlling principles have emerged. The States and school administrators have comprehensive authority, consistent with fundamental constitutional safeguards, to prescribe and control conduct in the schools. . . . Similarly, University administrators have the *responsibility* to control and regulate the conduct and behavior of students which tend to impede, obstruct or threaten the achievement of a University's educational goals. . . . This authority over the student, while comprehensive, is not absolute and a student's constitutional rights must be recognized and ". . . applied in light of the special characteristics of the school environment." *Tinker v. Des Moines Community School Dist.* . . ., 89 S.Ct. at 736. A student may express his opinions, even on controversial subjects, if he does so without materially or substantially interfering *with appropriate discipline* in the operation of the school, and without colliding with the rights of others. . . . Nevertheless, in or out of the University, the First Amendment does not require that persons with opinions or beliefs can express them at any time, and at any place, whenever and however and wherever they please. . . . Therefore, a State University, in order to create a suitable climate for study and to maintain appropriate discipline, may impose reasonable and non-discriminatory regulations of time, place and manner even on pure speech. See C. A. Wright, Constitution on the Campus, 22 *Vanderbilt Law Review* 1027, 1039 (1960). "The rights of freedom of assemblage and freedom of expression must not be exercised in such a way as to interfere with the operation of classrooms and laboratories, with the availability and use of libraries and other facilities, or with the conduct of the university's administrative responsibilities. Reasonable regulations to prevent such interference is clearly within the rule-making jurisdiction of the University." Sherry, Governance of University: Rules, Rights and Responsibilities, 54 *Calif. L.R.* 27 (1966). However, one point should be made perfectly clear! While freedom of expression and freedom of assembly are to be carefully protected from unwarranted University interference, *action* is quite different as it "carries no first amendment shield and can be regulated in any

way that the public helath, safety, morals, and welfare require."
Wright, *supra,* at 1039. In addition, certain forms of *conduct mixed
with speech* may be regulated or prohibited. "The most classic of
these was pointed out long ago by Mr. Justice Holmes: 'The most
stringent protection of free speech would not protect a man in falsely
shouting fire in a theatre and causing panic'." *Schenck v. United States,*
249 U.S. 47, 52, 39 S.Ct. 247, 249, 63 L.Ed. 470. . . . These limita-
tations, in some instances, may be more appropriate on a university
campus than in the non-university society because of the selective
purpose and the special characteristics of the school environment
referred to in Tinker. Finally, Courts do not and cannot intervene
in the resolution of conflicts which arise in the daily operation of
school systems and which do not directly and sharply implicate
basic constitutional values. . . . The judiciary must exercise restraint in questioning the wisdom of specific rules or the manner of
their application, since such matters are ordinarily the prerogatives
of school administrators rather than the Courts. . . . On the other
hand, the vigilant protection of constitutional freedom is nowhere
more vital than in the community of American schools. . . .

The important question for our purposes is whether the vagueness and overbreadth standard applies with equal force to student
regulations at a State University. The tenor of the cases appears to
recognize that the doctrine is applicable to student regulations, but
not with the same specificity that is required of State criminal statutes. Even the Opinion of Judge Doyle at the District Court level in
Soglin v. Kauffman, 295 F. Supp. 978 (W.D.Wisc. 1968), affirmed, 418
F.2d 163 (7th Cir. 1969), on which plaintiffs heavily rely, noted that
the doctrine applied "in some measure" to university regulation
and, on appeal, the Seventh Circuit Court of Appeals expressly held
that university codes of conduct are not required to satisfy the same
rigorous standards as criminal statutes: 418 F.2d at 168. . . . The
Report of the American Bar Association Commission on Campus
Government and Student Dissent (1970), advises against detailed
codes of conduct comparable to criminal statutes and recommends
rules which will provide fair notice of what is expected and what is
forbidden. Otherwise, the Commission fears such elaborate codes
may detract from the educational character of an academic institution and may inadvertently create an adversary relationship be-

tween school officials and students. The Eighth Circuit Court of Appeals suggests "flexibility and reasonable breadth, rather than meticulous specificity" and further observes, with reference to the ability of the body to whom the rules are directed to understand them, that "the college student . . . is appropriately expected to possess some minimum intelligence. . . ." *Esteban v. Central Missouri State College, supra,* at 1088. The regulation herein, therefore, will be read in the light of the principles enunciated above, viz., mindful of the comprehensive authority possessed by school officials to prescribe and control conduct in the schools, the need for flexibility and reasonable breadth in the promulgation of Rules of Conduct, the educational ends sought to be accomplished in a university setting, and the intellectual competency of the student body, is Section II(a) of the University Guide so vague and overbroad on its face as to deny fundamental constitutional safeguards to the plaintiffs? I hold that it is not. . . .

The Regulation excludes any *action* or combination of actions which *unreasonably* interferes with the operation of, and right of *access to*, physical accommodations used in the performance of the teaching, research, and administrative functions and related adjunct activities of the University, or infringes upon the rights of others to freely participate in its programs and services. What is unreasonable, much less unconstitutional, about a Regulation declaring physical accommodations used in the performance of teaching, research, and administrative functions out of bounds for such disruptive actions? *Whether it is speech-connected or stems soley from an aim to physically confiscate University property, when it becomes action that unreasonably interferes with the operation of certain essential functions of the University, it is not constitutionally protected and need not be tolerated.* The Regulation provides an adequate guide to the student of what is expected and what is forbidden. Even under the standard applicable to statutes generally, men of common intelligence would not *necessarily* guess at its meaning and differ as to its application and a *reasonable* application of its terms would not include conduct protected by the Constitution. . . .

The occasion to infringe upon the rights of others is more available in the University community, and especially in those facilities where study, concentration and attentiveness are so much more the order of the day, than in a non-university setting. A classroom where an instructor is lecturing interested students is entitled to at least as much protection as the theatre where the shouting of "fire" is not to be countenanced. Research functions similarly involve a tranquil, non-disruptive atmosphere wherein the work at hand can be appropriately accomplished. Administrative functions are usually confined and centralized and would involve the use of only a small part of university property. In order to function properly and to provide educational opportunity and appropriate atmosphere, school administrators must protect against unreasonable interference with the operation of these vital and sensitive facilities. That is what was done here in language that provides as much of a compass as a student should need to fairly notify him of what is expected and what is not. The Regulation here, Section II(a) of the University Guide, is reasonable, non-discriminatory, and sufficiently specific and necessary to fulfill the University mission. Plaintiff's contention that it is vague and overbroad is rejected. . . .

9

DORMITORY SEARCHES

The right of the people to be secure in their persons, houses, papers, and effects, against unreasonable searches and seizures shall not be violated and no Warrants shall issue, but upon probable cause, supported by Oath or affirmation, and particularly describing the place to be searched, and the persons or things to be seized.[1]

The constitutional prohibition against unreasonable searches and seizures had its immediate historical background in the colonial experience with Great Britain. Time and again the colonials complained against searches by English troops or revenue officers seeking evidence of smuggling, insurrection, or other crimes. The depth of feeling is reflected in the Fourth Amendment, quoted above.

The words of the Fourth Amendment must be read not by themselves but in the context of society's equally valid interest in law enforcement. As with many constitutional rights, its interpretation over the years represents an attempt at an accommodation between competing values. The most obvious value is, of course, that alluded to above, the right of a person to be secure in his own property.

The Fourth Amendment, and the personal rights which it secures, have a long history. At the very core stands the right of a man to retreat into his own home and there be free from unreasonable governmental intrusion.[2]

[1]U.S. Constitution, Amendment IV.

[2]*Silverman v. U.S.*, 365 U.S. 505, 511 (1961).

147

The protection afforded by this Amendment is effective not only against the federal government, but also against incursions by state authorities. Once again the interpretation of the Fourteenth Amendment expands a constitutional right to include actions by the individual states.

The general rule established by the Fourth Amendment is that there may be no search without a warrant, even if the police are reasonably sure in their own mind that a crime is being committed in a person's home or other sanctuary. The rationale is that the minor inconvenience of obtaining a warrant is of small matter when weighed against a person's right to personal security. Thus the police may not enter upon and search a room even if they smell the odor of burning opium.[3]

The protection is extended not only to the owner of the premises but also to lessees, guests in hotel rooms, offices, the apartment of a friend, and automobiles. The Supreme Court has refused to extend the doctrine to cover open fields around one's home, however.

The net effect of the Fourth Amendment is to require the police to secure a warrant if they wish to undertake a search. The warrant itself may be issued only upon "probable cause." This means that the law enforcement officer seeking a warrant from a magistrate must swear or affirm with some specificity to the incidents upon which he bases his judgment that there is probability of a crime and he must also specifically describe the premises to be searched.

There are certain exceptions to the requirement of a warrant. The most obvious occurs when the owner of the premises permits the search. This permission must be explicit and be given without intimidation or duress. The second exception is that law enforcement officers may search premises if the search is incident to a lawful arrest. The theory of this exception is that such authority is necessary in order that the officers may search to secure weapons that may be used to injure them or to effectuate an escape, or to prevent the destruction of evidence. In any case, if the accused later claims the search was illegal, the police have to show that the arrest itself was proper. If the officers did not have sufficient evidence to establish

[3] *Johnson v. U.S.*, 333 U.S. 10 (1948).

probable cause of a crime before the search, subsequent acquisition of evidence is inadmissable and the search will be declared improper.

The material on search and seizure outlined above represents the general criminal law doctrine in the field. The question obviously presents itself as to whether this doctrine is applicable in a college dormitory setting. In this connection it should be kept in mind that if the search is not proper, any evidence secured will not be admissable in court. The problem has obviously become one of increasing concern with the growth in the use of addictive drugs.

The courts have generally recognized that students who reside in on-campus dormitories have a special relationship with the institution. This special relationship grows out of a recognition of the college's obligation to promulgate and enforce reasonable regulations designed to protect campus order and discipline and to promote an environment conducive to the educational process. Accordingly, the courts recognize the right of the institution to promulgate regulations allowing a reasonable right of inspection. As one court has stated, students do not have the full rights of tenants but rather their rights "must yield to the extent that they would interfere with the institution's fundamental duty to operate the school as an educational institution. A reasonable right of inspection is necessary to the institution's performance of that duty even though it may infringe on the outer boundaries of a dormitory student's Fourth Amendment rights."[4] In the *Moore* case, the search was initiated by the college with reasonable cause and conducted by state narcotics agents, who were accompanied by the Dean of Men. A quantity of marijuana was discovered, and institutional discipline was imposed. The student brought an action in the federal court challenging the use of this evidence in the college disciplinary proceedings.

The principles of the *Moore* case indicate that whereas a student cannot be required to waive his Fourth Amendment rights, colleges may have catalog stipulations reserving the right to enter and inspect rooms. They may do this for purposes of safety or if they have a reasonable belief that the room is being used for illegal purposes or for activity that would otherwise seriously interfere with campus

[4]*Moore v. Student Affairs Committee,* 284 F. Supp. 725, 729 (1968).

discipline. This appears to be a standard lower than "probable cause" and one that is justified on the special necessities in the student-college relationship. Any evidence secured during such an inspection may be used against the student in university discipline proceedings.

From the foregoing it can be seen that the student-college position is very different from that of the individual and public law enforcement officers. It should be noted, however, that this difference is relevant only to university-student proceedings. A very different set of guidelines controls when one seeks to use such evidence in a criminal proceeding or when the university permits the police to enter a room to secure evidence for criminal prosecution. In these later instances, the Fourth Amendment protections are invoked and the courts have held that the principles of the *Moore* case are not applicable.

Judge Frank Johnson of the Federal Court in Alabama decided the *Moore* case in 1968. In 1970 he was presented with an appeal by students from Troy State University whose rooms were searched by narcotics agents accompanied by University officials.[5] In this case, however, the local police initiated the process by requesting the cooperation of the University in searching rooms where they believed narcotics would be found. After discovery of marijuana, the students were charged and convicted in the state criminal courts. The defendants appealed to the Federal Court, and the state used the Moore case as precedent.

Judge Johnson drew a distinction between the two cases and pointed out that the state's lack of probable cause in *Piazzola* could not be cured by the relaxed standards of *Moore*. The latter case was a school search for school purposes; the former, a police search for purposes of criminal prosecution. Here the Fourth Amendment is fully applicable. Thus the mere fact that the University reserved the right to inspect rooms for their own institutional purposes did not mean that it could exercise the right through police officers. This is an extension of the principle that when a party retains the right to inspect the premises of another for limited purposes, this right cannot be delegated to the police or used as consent for a police search.

---

[5]*Piazzola and Marinshaw v. Watkins,* 316 F. Supp. 624 (1970).

Similarly, the federal District Court in New York has disposed of the argument that a dormitory student through his relationship with the university has impliedly consented to their right to authorize a search by the police.

It offends reason and logic to suppose that a student will consent to an entry into his room designed to establish grounds on which to arrest him. Certainly there can be no rational claim that a student will self-consciously waive his constitutional rights to a lawful search and seizure. Finally, even if the doctrine of implied consent were imported into this case, the consent is given, not to police officials, but to the University and the latter cannot fragmentize, share, or delegate it.[6]

In summary, a student's room may be subject to search by university authorities under conditions that do not satisfy the requirements of the Fourth Amendment. Evidence secured thereby may be used only for institutional discipline, not in criminal proceedings. In order to be admissable in a court of competent jurisdiction, the evidence secured from a dormitory room must be acquired in full compliance with the requirements of the Fourth Amendment.

[6]*People v. Cohen,* 292 N.Y.2d 706 (1968).

Moore v. Student Affairs Committee of Troy State University

United States District Court, M.D. Alabama No. Div., 1968
284 F. Supp. 725.

JOHNSON, Chief Judge:

On February 28, 1968, plaintiff, Gregory Gordon Moore, was a student in good standing at Troy State University and resided in a dormitory on the campus which he rented from the school. A search of his room on that day, conducted by the Dean of Men and two agents of the State of Alabama Health Department, Bureau of Primary Prevention, in plaintiff's presence, revealed a substance which, upon analysis, proved to be marijuana. Following a hearing on March 27, 1968, by the Student Affairs Committee of Troy State University, plaintiff was "indefinitely suspended" from that institution on March 28. . . .

Plaintiff now seeks relief in this court. He seeks readmission as a student at Troy State University on the ground of denial of procedural due process in the proceedings which resulted in his suspension. He alleges the admission in the University's hearing of the evidence obtained through a search of his dormitory room violates his Fourth Amendment rights prohibiting illegal search and seizure.

On the morning of February 28, 1968, the Dean of Men of Troy State University was called to the office of the Chief of Police of Troy, Alabama, where a conference was held regarding "the possibility of there being marijuana on the campus." Two narcotics agents, the Chief of Police, and two students were present. A second meeting was held later that morning at which a list was procured of the names of students whose rooms the officers desired permission to search. This information came from unnamed but reliable informers. About 1 p.m. the officers received additional information that some of the subjects they were interested in were packing to leave the campus for a break following the end of an examination period. Upon receipt of this information, and fearing a "leak," two narcotics agents, accompanied by the Dean of Men, searched six dormitory rooms in two separate residence halls. The search of the room which plaintiff occupied alone occurred between approximately 2:30 and 2:45 p.m., in his presence, but without his permission.

At the second hearing before the Student Affairs Committee, the following stipulation was entered concerning the search:

That no search warrant was obtained in this case, that no consent to search was given by the defendant, that the search was not incidental to a legal arrest, that no other offense was committed by the defendant in the arresting officers' presence, that Troy State University had in force and effect at the time of the search and subsequent arrest of the defendant the following regulation, "The college reserves the right to enter rooms for inspection purposes. If the administration deems it necessary the room may be searched and the occupant required to open his personal baggage and any other personal material which is sealed." This language appears in the Troy State College current bulletin of the year 1967-68. The quoted language also appears . . . in the Troy State Bulletin for the year 1967-68. . . . This language also appears in the current publication of the Oracle, which is a student handbook. . . . This language further appears on the reverse side of a leaflet entitled "Residence Hall Policies" which is also made available to all students of Troy State University.

It is further stipulated that the defendant's room was searched at the invitation or consent of Troy State University by the law enforcement officials acting under the above quoted regulations.

The search revealed a matchbox containing a small amount of vegetable matter, which a state toxicologist who examined it testified was marijuana. All this testimony was received over plaintiff's objection that the evidence was seized as a result of a search in violation of the Fourth Amendment. He also challenges the constitutionality, facially and as applied, of the regulation under which the search was conducted.

This Court has previously expressed itself on the question of campus regulations, and the duty of school administrations to maintain order and discipline on their campuses in an environment suited to education, in *Dickey v. Alabama State Board of Education*, 273 F. Supp. 613, 617-618 (M.D.Ala. 1967):

This Court recognizes that the establishment of an educational program requires certain rules and regulations necessary for maintaining an orderly program and operating the institution in a manner conducive to learning. However, the school and school officials have always been bound by the requirement that the rules and regulations *must be reasonable*. [Emphasis in original.] Courts may only consider whether rules and regulations that are imposed by school authorities are a reasonable exercise of the power and discretion vested in those authorities. *Regulations and rules which are necessary in maintaining order and discipline are always considered reasonable.* . . . State school officials cannot infringe on their students' right of free and unrestricted expression as guaranteed by the Constitution of the United States where the exercise of such right does not "materially and substantially interfere with requirements of appropriate discipline in the operation of the school." *Burnside v. Byars*, 363 F. 2d 744 (5th Cir. 1966). [Emphasis added.]

. . . College students who reside in dormitories have a special relationship with the college involved. Insofar as the Fourth Amendment affects that relationship, it does not depend on either a general theory of the right of privacy or on traditional property concepts. The college does not stand, strictly speaking, *in loco parentis* to its students, nor is their relationship purely contractual in the traditional sense. The relationship grows out of the peculiar and sometimes the seemingly competing interests of college and student. A student naturally has the right to be free of unreasonable search and seizure, and a tax-supported public college may not compel a "waiver" of that right as a condition precedent to admission. The college, on the other hand, has an "affirmative obligation" to promulgate and to enforce reasonable regulations designed to protect campus order and discipline and to promote an environment consistent with the educational process. The validity of the regulation authorizing search of dormitories thus does not depend on whether a student "waives" his right to Fourth Amendment protection or on whether he has "contracted" it away; rather, its validity is determined by whether the regulation is a reasonable exercise of the college's supervisory duty. In other words, if the regulation—or, in the absence of a regulation, the action of the college authorities—is necessary in aid of the basic responsibility of the institution regarding discipline and the maintenance of an "educational atmosphere," then it will be presumed facially reasonable despite the fact that it may infringe to some extent on the outer bounds of the Fourth Amendment rights of students. . . .

The student is subject only to reasonable rules and regulations, but his rights must yield to the extent that they would interfer with the institution's fundamental duty to operate the school *as an edu-cational institution.* A reasonable right of inspection is necessary to the institution's performance of that duty even though it may infringe on the outer boundaries of a dormitory student's Fourth Amendment rights. . . . The regulation of Troy State University in issue here is thus facially reasonable.

The regulation was reasonable applied in this case. The constitutional boundary line between the right of the school authorities to search and the right of a dormitory student to privacy must be based on a reasonable belief on the part of the college authorities that a student is using a dormitory room for a purpose which is illegal or which would otherwise seriously interfere with campus discipline. Upon this submission, it is clear that such a belief existed in this case.

This standard of "reasonable cause to believe" to justify a search by college administrators—even where the sole purpose is to seek evidence of suspected violations of law—is lower than the constitutionally protected criminal law standard of "probable cause." This is true because of the special necessities of the student-college relationship and because college disciplinary proceedings are not criminal proceedings in the constitutional sense. . . .

Assuming that the Fourth Amendment applied to college disciplinary proceedings, the search in this case would not be in violation of it. It is settled law that the Fourth Amendment does not prohibit reasonable searches when the search is conducted by a superior charged with a responsibility of maintaining discipline and order or of maintaining security. A student who lives in a dormitory on campus which he "rents" from the school waives objection to any reasonable searches conducted pursuant to reasonable and necessary regulations such as this one. . . .

In accordance with the foregoing, it is the order, judgment and decree of this Court that plaintiff's claims for relief be and are, in each instance, hereby denied. It is ordered that this cause be and the same is hereby dismissed. . . .

Piazzola and Marinshaw v. Watkins

United States District Court, M.D. Alabama, N.D., 1970
316 F. Supp. 624.

JOHNSON, Chief Judge:

The petitioners were indicted by a grand jury of Pike County, Alabama, for the offense of illegal possession of marijuana. After pleas of not guilty were interposed, trials were had, and petitioner Piazzola was convicted on April 25, 1968. The convictions were affirmed by the Alabama Court of Criminal Appeals. The matter is presented to this Court upon a habeas corpus petition filed April 24, 1970. The basis for the petition is that the convictions violate the Fourth Amendment to the Constitution of the United States. . . .

On the morning of February 28, 1968, the Dean of Men of Troy State University was called to the office of the Chief of Police of Troy, Alabama, to discuss the "drug problem" at the University. Two State narcotic agents and two student informers from Troy State University were also present. Later on that same day, the Dean of Men was called to the city police station for another meeting; at this time he was informed by the officers that they had sufficient evidence that marijuana was in the dormitory rooms of certain Troy State students and that they desired the cooperation of University officials in searching these rooms. The police officers were advised by the Dean of Men that they would receive the full cooperation of the University officials in searching for the marijuana. The informers, whose identities have not yet been disclosed, provided the police officers with names of students whose rooms were to be searched. Still later on that same day (which was during the week of final examinations at the University and was to be followed by a week-long holiday) the law enforcement officers, accompanied by some of the University officials, searched six or seven dormitory rooms located in two separate residence halls. The rooms of Piazzola and Marinshaw were searched without search warrants and without their consent. Present during the search of the room occupied by Marinshaw were two State narcotic agents, the University security officer, and a counselor of the residence hall where Marinshaw's room was located. Piazzola's room was searched twice. Present during the first search were two State narcotic agents and a University official; no evidence was found at this time. The second search of

Piazzola's room, which disclosed the incriminating evidence, was conducted solely by the State and city police officials.

At the time of the seizure the University had in effect the following regulation:

The college reserves the right to enter rooms for inspection purposes. If the administration deems it necessary, the room may be searched and the occupant required to open his personal baggage and any other personal material which is sealed.

Each of the petitioners was familiar with this regulation. After the search of the petitioners' rooms and the discovery of the marijuana, they were arrested, and the State criminal prosecutions and convictions ensued. The basic question presented is whether the evidence that formed the basis for the petitioners' convictions and present incarceration was obtained as a result of an unreasonable search and seizure within the meaning of the Fourth Amendment to the Constitution of the United States. As justification for the search and seizure, the respondents rely almost entirely upon this Court's opinion in *Moore v. Student Affairs Committee of Troy State University*, 284 F. Supp. 725 (M.D. Ala.). The *Moore* case involved judicial review of the constitutional validity of University administrative proceedings which resulted in the suspension of Gary Moore from Troy University. The suspension in the *Moore* case was based upon a search of Moore's dormitory room by University officials and the discovery of marijuana in his room. In *Moore*, this Court emphasized:

A student naturally has the right to be free of unreasonable searches and seizures, and a tax-supported public college may not compel a "waiver" of that right as a condition precedent to admission.

Upon the facts presented in *Moore*, this Court held that the University regulation authorizing the search of dormitory rooms was a reasonable exercise of University supervisory duties. . . .

This Court does not find *Moore* applicable in the case *sub judice*. Here, the search was instigated and in the main executed by State police and narcotic bureau officials. The only part the University officials played in the search of the petitioners' dormitory rooms was at the request of and under the direction of the State law enforcement officers. Under such circumstances the State of Alabama, upon the petitioners' motion to suppress, had the burden of showing probable cause for the search of petitioners' rooms. The standard of "reasonable cause to believe" laid down by this Court in *Moore* as a justification for a search by college officials that resulted in school disciplinary proceedings cannot be the justification for a search by a police officer for the sole purpose of gathering evidence for criminal prosecutions. . . .

No other evidence was offered by the State in justification of the search, except that the officers "had information," that they believed that information, and that, implied by the testimony, there were some unnamed informers whose information or credibility as informers was never discussed.

The State's evidence on the question of probable cause failed completely. Under the circumstances that existed in this case, in order to establish probable cause the State police officers must give the underlying facts or circumstances upon which they base their conclusions. Furthermore, when officers contend that they searched upon information from an informer, they must show that the informer was reliable, and the evidence must also reflect some factual basis for the informant's conclusions. . . .

The State argues, in support of its warrantless search, that the petitioners consented to the search indirectly by reason of the University regulation. This argument cannot stand. As stated earlier, this was not a University initiated search for University purposes, but rather a police initiated search for criminal prosecution purposes. The fact that the University officials agreed to the search gives it no validity. As this Court emphasized in *Moore*, students and their college share a special relationship, which gives to the college certain special rights including the right to enter into and inspect the rooms of its students under certain situations. However, the fact that the college has this right—for a restricted purpose—does not mean that the college may exercise the right by admitting a third party. . . .

This means, therefore, that, even though the special relationship that existed between these petitioners and Troy University officials conferred upon the University officials the right to enter and search petitioners' dormitory rooms, that right cannot be expanded and used for purposes other than those pertaining to the special relationship. The right conferred by reason of the special relationship must be very narrowly construed, and with such a construction the University's right to enter and search could not in this instance be delegated to the State criminal investigators. This Court in *Moore* emphasized that the Court was setting the outer limits of University authority, stating:

[A] student is subject only to reasonable rules and regulations, but his rights must yield to the extent that they would interfere with the institution's fundamental duty to operate the school *as an educational institution.*

This distinction is not one of form over substance. The distinction lies in the "special relationship" existing between the college and the student and the purposes for which the search is conducted.

Since there was no warrant, no probable cause for searching without a warrant, and no waiver or consent, the search of petitioners' dormitory rooms by State law enforcement officers, including narcotic agents and Troy city police officers, on February 28, 1968, was in violation of the petitioners' rights as guaranteed by the Fourth Amendment to the Constitution of the United States. It follows that the convictions of the petitioners, having been based solely upon the fruits of such search, are likewise illegal and cannot stand. Accordingly, it is the

Order, judgment and decree of this Court that the conviction of Frank Piazzola on April 25, 1968, and the conviction of Terrance Marinshaw on April 26, 1968, both in the Circuit Court of Pike County, Alabama, which convictions form the basis for the present incarceration of each, be and each of said convictions is hereby set aside. It is further

Ordered that Frank Piazzola and Terrance Marinshaw be released immediately by the State authorities now holding them in custody pursuant to said convictions.

10

MISCELLANY

Several areas of student rights can be treated in less than chapter length. This last chapter will deal with these areas, which include dormitories, student organizations and fraternities, payment of fees, student health, appearance, and claims against an educational institution.

DORMITORIES

Aside from the Fourth Amendment questions of search and seizure, which are dealt with above (Chapter 9), there are several issues pertaining to student dormitories that merit consideration. The authority of state legislatures to build dormitories at state colleges and universities has often been questioned in the courts. The consistent judicial answer to this query has been that such authority does exist.[1] Providing dormitories for students is considered part of the educational function of the state and therefore well within the scope of its authority.

The crux of most legal problems involving dormitories deals with regulations promulgated for their use. Unless there is an abuse of discretion by the college in such matters, the courts will follow a hands-off-policy. Furthermore, courts will refuse to substitute

---

[1]*Pyeatte v. Board of Regents of the University of Oklahoma*, 102 F. Supp. 407 (Okla. 1951), affirmed 342 U.S. 936 (1952).

their judgment unless there has been unreasonable and arbitrary conduct by a college. In a case brought by a mother of a female student attending Vassar College, the rules allowing relaxed parietal (visiting) hours were challenged.[2] The new regulations had been approved overwhelmingly by the student body of the college. The Court dismissed the mother's complaint and observed:

In academic communities greater freedoms may prevail than in society at large and the subtle fixing of these limits should, to a great degree, be left to the educational institution itself. . . . The judiciary must exercise restraint in questioning the wisdom of specific rules or the manner of their application, since such matters are ordinarily in the prerogative of school administrators rather than the courts. . . .

The Court concluded:

It is the privilege of a college, through its Student Government Association, to promulgate and enforce rules and regulations for the social conduct of students without judicial interference. . . .

Another point often contested in reference to dormitories is the right of the college to make it mandatory for matriculating students to live in campus housing. There have been several decisions dealing with this question. The general rule acknowledges the right of state colleges to require undergraduate students to live in college dormitories.[3] There are, however, clear exceptions to the rule. For instance, married students are not compelled to live on campus. The reason for this is that public policy encourages married couples to stay together. To establish a contrary requirement would lend itself to the separation of man and wife, and be inconsistent with the mores of our society.[4]

An earlier case involved the question of whether girls at a state college who are unmarried and under 21 years of age can be required, constitutionally, to support a college housing system.[5] The facts in the case reveal that the school was having trouble in filling

---

[2] *Jones v. Vassar College*, 299 N.Y.S.2d 283 (1969).

[3] *Pratz et al. v. Louisiana Polytechnic Institute et al.*, 316 F. Supp. 872 (1970), affirmed 401 U.S. 951 (1971).

[4] Clarence J. Bakken, *The Legal Basis for College Student Personnel Work*, second edition (Washington, D.C.: The American College Personnel Association, 1968), p. 20.

[5] *Mollere et al. v. Southeastern Louisiana College*, 304 F. Supp. 826 (1969).

its dormitories. As a result, insufficient funds were available to reduce its dormitory debt obligation. To meet this problem, the college promulgated a rule to require unmarried women students under 21 not living with their parents or with a close relative to live in campus residence halls unless an exception was granted by the Dean of Women. Similar provision was made for male members of the freshman class. The rule was challenged, and the court ruled in favor of the plaintiff-students. The opinion upheld the principle that a college has a right, as part of its educational function, to require students to live in dormitories. Notwithstanding, the Court took pains to show that in this case some students and not others were being penalized for the sake of meeting a debt of the institution. It said:

> . . . in effect, it is a requirement that some students musy pay while others need not. . . . The burden of expense is falling on some but not on others.

The decision found the dormitory requirement in question to be discriminatory and impermissible under the Fourteenth Amendment. The point made in the case is an important one. When a college or university is faced with a financial debt, any assessment placed on the students to reduce the debt must be placed on all of them or on none of them. Certain selected students, no matter how they are selected, cannot be compelled to pay. Simply put—it is a matter of "all or nothing at all."

Another dormitory issue involves student civil rights. Separate housing for Negro students in college dormitories brings this question into sharp focus. In the late 1960's, black students at Northwestern University, Antioch, and other colleges sought the assignment of separate campus housing for Negro students.[6] In response, the United States Department of Health, Education, and Welfare opposed the idea of segregated dormitories. It threatened the termination of all federal funds to any institution of higher education that supported such a plan. H.E.W. took the position that black dormitories were inconsistent with Title VI of The Civil Rights Act of 1964, which prohibits discrimination on the grounds of race, color, or national origin in any federal program. A memorandum

---

[6]*Washington Post,* June 2, 1968, p. A6, and March 6, 1969, pp. A1 and A11.

from the Office for Civil Rights of the Department of Health, Education, and Welfare on this point appears to have laid to rest the question regarding the legality of black dormitories.[7] This significant memo also prohibited black studies programs that exclude students on the basis of race, color, or national origin.

Despite the impact of the 1969 HEW memorandum, there does remain an unanswered question that begs for judicial determination. It involves the legality of residence buildings belonging to fraternities and sororities with restrictive membership provisions located on public university property. It would appear that such an arrangement is inconsistent with modern constitutional principles, and, unless the government acts to eliminate such arrangements, litigation of the issue may result.

[7]Memorandum to Presidents of Institutions of Higher Education participating in Federal Assistance Programs from the Office of the Secretary, Department of Health, Education, and Welfare, March 1969:

It has come to our attention that many colleges and universities are initiating special programs for Negro and other minority group students. The programs range from those that will help the minority student who may have unique problems to those that look to the establishment of a separate school on campus solely for the use of the minority student. We wish to make you aware that, for whatever minority group is sought to be served, certain actions on the part of an institution of higher education constitute a violation of compliance requirements of Title VI of the Civil Rights Act of 1964.

1. Separate Housing for Students Based on Race—All housing which is owned, operated or supported by the institution or a public agency must be available to all students without regard to race, color or national origin and assignment to such housing must be made in a nondiscriminatory manner.

2. Separate Social Activity Space—Where the institution donates or otherwise makes available institution-owned facilities or land for student use or activities or where it provides funds or other financial assistance to acquire or operate facilities for such activities, it must be assured that the activities are to be operated without discrimination based on race, color or national origin.

3. Separate Colleges, Schools or Institutes—Every service and benefit offered by the institution to students must be open and available to all students without regard to race, color or national origin.

The Office for Civil Rights has encouraged, and will continue to support, the institutions' efforts to recruit, enroll and matriculate "high risk" students, minority or otherwise, and to offer such students a well-rounded and relevant social and academic environment on campus. However, we must enforce the congressional intent of prohibiting Federally-assisted institutions from offering services and benefits which result in segregation on the basis of race. We realize that each institution is confronted by separate and unique problems, and we are prepared to discuss the legality of any program with individual college representatives.

STUDENT ORGANIZATIONS

Extracurricular activities are an integrated part of student life. Although these outside-the-classroom activities are not, in most cases, considered academic in nature, they do have an important influence on the intellectual and social development of the student. Their contribution to the total college experience makes them highly valuable, and their existence is encouraged by student and institution alike. Notwithstanding this shared enthusiasm, student and school policies frequently conflict concerning student activities. Certain practices of an organization may be found undesirable or the establishment of a particular club may be thought inconsistent with the purposes of the college. It is at this point that the rights of the students clash with the rules and regulations of the institution, and an understanding of the law on this point is important to all parties.

Here again it is necessary to distinguish between public and private schools. When public colleges and universities are involved, they are subject to the control of the legislature. The legislative authority and responsibility may be delegated, and often are, to the institution's trustees or to the institution's administration and faculty. Under this principle, college and university authorities may make all the rules and regulations for the orderly management of the institution, which include supervision of the extracurricular activities of students.[8] In the private sector, the right to adopt suitable standards governing student life is acknowledged, if the rules are reasonable and not arbitrary.[9] There must be a clear abuse of authority by the private institutions before the courts will intervene.

In cases involving student organizations, the courts must strike a delicate balance between the institution's responsibility to maintain orderly operation and the student's freedom of association. On this point, the *Report of the American Bar Association Commission on Campus Government and Student Dissent* is helpful. It commented:

Students should be free to organize and to participate in voluntary associations of their own choosing subject to university regulations insuring that

[8]15 *American Jurisprudence* 2d 608 § 22 (Rochester, N.Y.: The Lawyers Co-Operative Publishing Co., 1964).

[9]*Ibid.*

such associations are neither discriminatory in their treatment of other members of the academic community nor operated in a manner which substantially interferes with the rights of others.[10]

This statement of the A.B.A. Commission is illustrated by two federal cases. The first is the *American Civil Liberties Union v. Radford College.*[11] Students at Radford College attempted to register a campus chapter of the ACLU. The students complied with all the existing college regulations for registration. After a long period of bureaucratic delay, the students were informed that their request for recognition had been denied.

The United States District Court for the Western District of Virginia entertained the case and ruled for the students. Initially the judge acknowledged that student organizations do not have an unqualified prerogative to be recognized by school administrations. It admitted that college officials have a wide discretion in this area, and their decisions must rest on what is most compatible with the school's educational objectives. Nevertheless, students do not discard their constitutional rights when they matriculate. In those instances when public institutions open their facilities to some organizations, they must be made available to other groups unless there is a clear and definite danger that violence or unlawful means will be used to accomplish the organization's goals. The court found that the ACLU did not present any such danger, and therefore should be recognized by Radford College.

The second case is *Healy v. James.*[12] It proves to be a highly important decision because of its direct bearing on the organization known as the Students for a Democratic Society.

Healy involved the request of students at Central Connecticut State College for recognition of a local chapter of SDS. Consistent with established procedure at the college, the students submitted their application for recognition to the Dean's office. The applicants took pains to explain that the chapter was not under the dictates of

[10]Chicago: American Bar Association and American Bar Foundation, 1970, p. 11.

[11]315 F. Supp. 893 (1970).

[12]40 *U.S. Law Week* 4887 (June 26, 1972).

any national organization. The matter was eventually referred to the Student Personnel Committee, an advisory group whose function it was to provide an informal review and to recommend policies concerning student affairs. The Committee, after deliberating, voted to recommend to the college president that the SDS Chapter be given official recognition as a campus organization. Despite the recommendation of the committee, the college president turned the request down and denied   recognition. The basis for the decision rested on the President's belief that the local chapter adhered "to at least some of the major tenets of the national organization." Furthermore, he found the published aims and philosophy of the Students for a Democratic Society, which included disruption and violence, to be contrary to the approved policy of the college.

Following the President's decision, the petitioning students brought an action in the Federal District Court to restrain the College from denying recognition. The Court ruled that the students were denied a hearing on their petition for recognition, and ordered an evidentiary hearing by the College in order to give the petitioners adequate opportunity to be heard. (A formal hearing was not provided in the first instance when the request for recognition was made.) In all cases, a timely hearing should be afforded those submitting the petition for recognition.[13]

An important point was made when the ruling observed that a college administrator does not have the liberty to go outside the group's application to make a personal finding. In the case, the president had not accepted the Committee's recommendation to grant recognition. On the contrary, he made his own independent conclusion and denied the students' petition for recognition, based on his own private and independent conclusions. The Court did not find this procedure acceptable. It pointed out that at least a minimal hearing was necessary. If this step was not observed, it added, "any political group, no matter what its stated purpose, could be summarily denied recognition on the personal whim of the deciding authority."

Notwithstanding the court's order for a hearing, a lengthy deci-

[13]311 F. Supp. 1275, 1281–82 (Conn. 1970).

sion was handed down dealing with the right of student groups to organize on campus. The opinion reflected much of the reasoning in *Radford.* It recognized the right of colleges to regulate social organizations and the principle that no student group is entitled, per se, to official college recognition. It observed that if a group threatens the academic and other stated purposes of the institution, denial of recognition by the college will not be interfered with by the courts.

Subsequently and consistent with the court order, Central Connecticut State College conducted an evidentiary hearing. Upon conclusion of the proceedings, the college president once again denied the local chapter of SDS's request for recognition. The case was once again brought before the United States District Court. In a second opinion, Judge E. Clarie upheld the President's ruling and said:

> The evidence clearly and unequivocally discloses that the philosophy and purpose of the national organization advocate the violent overthrow of existing government institutions, through the medium of disruptive anarchistic force. The College President responsibly concluded that "recognition of such a group would be contrary to the philosophy and lawful mission of this College." This Court finds that his decision was validly arrived at and violated no constitutional rights of the plaintiffs under the first and fourteenth amendments to the federal constitution.[14]

This case was appealed, and Judge Clarie's decision was upheld by the United States Circuit Court of Appeals,[15] but overruled by the United States Supreme Court.[16] The Supreme Court stated that recognition must be granted as long as the organization agrees to abide by the rules of the institution.

It is clear that colleges do have the right to exercise strong restraints when organizations and groups seriously threaten to undermine the educational goals of the institution. Nevertheless, we know from *Radford* and *Healy* that this right must be exercised within the restraints of the Fourteenth Amendment. *Ex parte* decisions denying recognition are strictly forbidden by the court. Notice and an im-

[14]Healy v. James, 319 F. Supp. 113, 117 (Conn. 1970).
[15]445 F.2d 1122 (July 15, 1971).
[16]40 *U.S. Law Week* 4887 (June 26, 1972).

partial and adequate hearing with sufficient safeguards to assure fairness are required to ensure the equally important right of students to organize and to associate freely.

FRATERNITIES

A form of student organization is the fraternity or sorority. For more than a century, fraternity membership on the college campus has raised legal questions; this is no less true today. But the current issues deal primarily with racial and religious discrimination practiced by some fraternities, whereas earlier cases were concerned with the larger question of whether an individual had the right to join a fraternal organization on campus.

The wide popularity of fraternities and sororities provides solid indication of their historic and current acceptance on the American college campus. Likewise, judicially, Greek letter societies have been found to be lawful activities and legally acceptable to the courts.[17] This does not imply, however, that fraternities and sororities have not been banned or prohibited. A leading case and one still considered to represent best the right to prohibit fraternities is *Waugh v. Board of Trustees of the University of Mississippi.*[18] This United States Supreme Court case upheld the authority of the trustees of the University of Mississippi to require all students to promise not to join a fraternity. The Court's reasoning emphasized that students do not have unlimited rights and it added that students attending public universities are recipients of free education, and as a result must be ready to yield some of their liberties, especially when a particular activity may be considered "inimical to the discipline" of the university. In 1866, it had been decided that students attending a private college did not have a right to fraternity membership.[19]

Although the *Waugh* holding remains an authoritive source on the right of colleges and universities to prohibit fraternities, sororities, and secret societies, the reasoning in support of the decision is questionable in a modern context, especially in view of the Supreme

[17]*State of Georgia et al. v. Davidson,* 198 Ga. 27 (1944).

[18]237 U.S. 589 (1915). Also see *Satan Fraternity v. Board of Public Instruction,* 156 Fla. 222 (1945).

[19]*People ex rel. Pratt v. Wheaton College,* 40 Ill. 186 (1866).

Court's ruling in *Healy v. James*. Few would agree that the student must surrender a portion of his liberties to attend a public college. attendance in some form can be a normal and reasonable expectation for any high school graduate. To imply that an individual must sacrifice his or her legal rights in order to attend a public college is totally unacceptable in terms of contemporary reasoning.

A more difficult problem is a school's position when dealing with a fraternity or sorority that has discriminatory membership provisions in its charter or by-laws. The question succinctly put— can a public institution of higher learning deprive an individual of his right to freedom of association by imposing regulations that prohibit an organization using university facilities from denying membership on the grounds of race, color, religion, or national origin?

Several cases provide adequate lines to answer at least part of the foregoing question. In *Sigma Chi Fraternity v. the Regents of the University of Colorado,*[20] the court held that a resolution by the Board of Regents of the University placing any "fraternity, social organization, or other student group" on probation for denying membership to any person because of race, color, or religion was valid.

Two New York cases recognize the same right of university trustees or regents to regulate fraternal or social organization membership.[21] These decisions uphold the right of a university's governing board to ban fraternal organizations. In finding the board's action valid, the court ruled that there was no violation of the civil rights of the members.

The rulings in these cases contrast with a principle enunciated by the United States Supreme Court in *NAACP v. Alabama ex rel. Patterson.*[22] In that case, the Court recognized the privilege to unite for the purpose of advancing "political, economic, religious or cultural matters." Moreover, it found that this freedom to associate for the advancement of beliefs and ideas is a liberty protected by the Due Process clause of the Fourteenth Amendment. There is some debate

[20]258 F. Supp. 515 (1966).

[21]*Webb v. State University of New York,* 125 F. Supp. 910 (N.Y. 1954), appeal dismissed 348 U.S. 867 (1954); and *Beta Sigma Rho, Inc. v. Moore,* 261 N.Y.S.2d 658 (1965).

[22]357 U.S. 449 (1958).

in legal circles[23] as to whether this ruling applies to college fraternities. The issue remains unsettled because no case has been decided on this precise point.

PAYMENT OF FEES

The collection and use of student activity fees are often the source of friction between students and administration. As a general rule, either the state legislature or the governing board may establish an amount for which each student is to be assessed.[24] Fees have been authorized for buildings, health services, student unions, and miscellaneous student services.[25] As long as the fee is reasonable and used for purposes within the general framework of the authority of the collecting body, the courts will not interfere.[26]

Once a fee for student activities has been collected, the matter of how it is to be spent becomes important. Although students have the right to make expenditures, does this imply total control over the monies? The statutes and regulations governing the institution must be examined carefully before venturing an answer. As a general rule, students do not have complete control over the expenditures of fees earmarked for student activities. In fact, disbursements may be made only in accordance with the purposes permitted by the board of trustees.[27]

An interesting illustration of this problem arose in Connecticut. The State Attorney General was requested to give his advice regarding the legality of an off-campus program sponsored by student funds. It appears that the Student Senate at Central Connecticut State College allocated $3,425.25 of its funds for a breakfast program for needy children. The question was raised whether the Student Senate had the authority to make such use of funds collected through student fees. In part, the pertinent legislation says:

[23] 39 *University of Colorado Law Review* 149 (1966–67), "Freedom of Association—Right of State University to Regulate Fraternity Membership Standards."

[24] Bakken, *Legal Basis for College Student Personnel Work,* p. 27.

[25] *Ibid.*

[26] *Rainey et al. v. Malone,* 141 S.W.2d 713 (Tex. 1940).

[27] *Stringer v. Gould et al.,* 314 N.Y.S.2d 309 (1970).

The management of such funds may be under the control of students, . . . but shall be under the supervision of the administrative head of the institution. . . .[28]

Furthermore, it adds that funds derived from student fees may be used only ". . . for the benefit of the . . . students of such institutions. . . ."[29]

The Attorney General ruled that the contemplated expenditure by the Student Senate would not be lawful. He commented:

. . . we must conclude that while the intent of the Student Senate was most laudable, nevertheless, the Student Senate is charged with the responsibility to disburse these funds only for the benefit of the students of Central Connecticut State College and further, that the college administration is charged with the supervisory responsibilities, which include the determination that any programs receiving support from such funds are in fact for the benefit of students.[30]

STUDENT HEALTH

Seldom is there specific authority granted to a public college or university to provide health services for its students. Generally it is assumed that this authority is granted in the general delegation of powers and responsibilities to operate the institution. In most, if not all, residential colleges, medical facilities are provided as part of the general operation of the institution.[31] Medical facilities and services are considered the responsibility of college officials, for by tradition they have been expected to oversee the health needs of their students.[32] In conjunction with this trust to look after student health, most institutions require at the time of the student's admission evidence of a physical examination. In addition, students may be required to have certain vaccinations or immunization shots.

On occasion a student will refuse to comply with a medical requirement for a physical examination or vaccination. In both

[28]Connecticut General Statutes 4-54.

[29]*Ibid.*, 4-52.

[30]Letter dated January 28, 1971, from Robert K. Killian, State Attorney General, to F. Don James, President, Central Connecticut State College.

[31]Bakken, *Legal Basis for College Student Personnel Work,* p. 31.

[32]*Ibid.*

the public[33] and private[34] sectors, colleges and universities usually have the right to demand student compliance. Failure of the student to meet this requirement can lead to the denial of admission. When there are proven religious reasons for refusing to have a vaccination, however, courts usually will not require the student to undergo a medical procedure contrary to his religious tenets.[35] Nevertheless, there are authorities who hold differently on this point and feel that the student should meet the medical requirements set down for all students. Their adamant position is rooted in concern for the good health of the entire student body. To have one person or few not conform could conceivably lead to a health hazard.[36]

APPEARANCE

The superficially most distinctive difference between male youth of today and of a generation ago is clearly dress style. One need only look at a vintage movie for dramatic evidence of this statement. White bucks have given way to sandals, khakis to levis, and the crew cut to an endless assortment of head and facial hair that render rather trite the muttonchops of a century ago. Whether this penchant for follicle finery is attributable to the inflationary spiral of the costs for tonsorial services, a desire for personal expression, or a generational rebellion against parental tastes need not concern us here. The fact is that we have entered an era of locks and beards. This increasing growth of youthful face fauna has not been unopposed. Indeed, more than one "mature" adult has purported to have discovered a corollary between long hair and homosexuality, drugs, rebellion, violence, etc.

In particular, certain school administrators have viewed the changing appearance of the students as not only a violation of good taste, but also a threat to the order and decorum of their institution. Accordingly, codes of dress and appearance have been formulated,

---

[33]Newton Edwards, *The Courts and the Public Schools* (Chicago: The University of Chicago Press, 1955), pp. 571-586.

[34]*John B. Stetson University v. Hunt*, 88 Fla. 510 (1925).

[35]*Kolbeck v. Kramer et al.*, 84 New Jersey Super. 569 (1964), affirmed 46 N.J. 46 (1965).

[36]*State ex rel. Holcomb v. Armstrong*, 39 Washington 2d 860 (1952).

designed to ensure that students conform to certain styles of dress and appearance. The most common feature of these codes has been a general requirement that hair not extend over the collars and that flambuoyant beards or sideburns not be permitted. The authority of school administrators to impose such codes has been questioned on a number of occasions.

The 1966 case of *Ferrill v. Dallas Independent School District*[37] is typical. In this case the students concerned were members of a musical group and claimed that it was necessary for them to maintain their Beatle-style haircuts in order to have a successful professional career. The federal court upheld the school's right to impose such restrictions. The court reasoned that the educational purposes of the school required the enactment of reasonable regulations to ensure individual development as well as an academic atmosphere. The court stated that "the rights of other students, and the interest of teachers, administrators, and the community at large are paramount: ". . . one of the most important aims of the school should be to educate the individual to live successfully with other people in a democracy."[38] This thinking is typical of earlier decisions upholding the right of school officials to enact dress and appearance codes. In general, the courts following this view emphasized the discretion of school authorities in establishing guidelines to ensure a minimum of disturbance and an academic atmosphere.

Not all courts adopted this liberal view of school administrators' authority. In a 1969 case in Wisconsin, Judge Doyle stated that "freedom to wear one's hair at a certain length or to wear a beard is constitutionally protected, even though it expresses nothing but individual taste."[39] The court asserted that any time the state attempts to regulate individual freedom, it must bear a substantial burden to justify its action in terms of the health, physical danger, or distraction of others. In this case there was no direct testimony that the plaintiff's long hair caused any distraction, nor were there presented any empirical studies to indicate such probability. In the Judge's view, the defendants failed to present evidence showing any

[37]261 F. Supp. 545.
[38]*Ibid.*, at 552.
[39]*Breen v. Kahl*, 296 F. Supp. 702, 706 (1969).

connection between long hair and academic atmosphere. He ordered the students reinstated. A similar result has been reached with students on a college level who insisted on maintaining pageboy hair cuts as part of their image as members of a musical group.[40]

These rulings seem to imply that under certain circumstances restrictions on grooming might be deemed appropriate. Apparently what the administrators must show is that there is a direct relationship between allegedly bizarre personal appearance and the decorus atmosphere deemed essential for an educational institution. Thus an institution may prevail if it can demonstrate that long hair, for instance, has continually led to disruptive reaction on the part of other students, which in turn has resulted in impairment of the educational process.

The dangerous tendency of such logic is that the legality of a regulation is tested not by any constitutional standard but by the reactions of others to it. Constitutionality by majority rule is a rather unique approach. At least one federal court has recognized these implications. In the 1969 case *Richards v. Thurston*,[41] the court refused to recognize any inherent authority for a school administrator to suspend a student whose hair style has been deemed untidy. In fact, the judge said that this matter of personal appearance was a constitutionally protected right. He went on and specifically overruled a case that emphasized disruptive reactions, stating that a person cannot be restrained from performing a lawful act merely because hostile individuals or groups might cause a disturbance.

In general, then, the trend has been to recognize personal clothing and style as a constitutionally protected right. Although an occasional case may uphold appearance codes on a showing of disruptive influence, the reasoning of the *Richards* case appears more sound.

There would seem to be an exception to the principles outlined above in the case of athletics. It has been recognized that participation in athletics can be a valuable part of the educational process and, accordingly, that students should be excluded only on the basis of competitive merit. Such an approach would be in keeping with

---

[40]*Zachry v. Brown*, 299 F. Supp. 1360 (1967).
[41]304 F. Supp. 449 (1969).

the principles already discussed for personal appearance. One of the purposes of athletics, however, is competition. Accordingly, if it can be shown that some aspect of a person's appearance affects his safety or ability to perform, the institution may require change. For instance, a football coach would be well within his rights to prohibit the wearing of beards or long hair that would prevent proper fitting of a protective helmet. Similarly, long hair for a swimmer could be unacceptable, in that it might inhibit his speed. It would seem that in each case, however, since there is an infringement on personal freedom, the burden would be upon the institution to show that there is a reasonable relationship between the requirements of the coach and the safety and ability of his athletes to perform. In line with the *Richards* case, it would not appear that the coach's insistence that a code was necessary to promote discipline would in itself be sufficient.

CLAIMS AGAINST AN EDUCATIONAL INSTITUTION

Whether one likes it or not, our society has progressed far beyond any mythical state of nature where individual differences were easily settled in a face-to-face encounter. Today's complex social arrangements require that there be some ultimate arbiter. In a civilized society this function is served by a judicial system. Thus, when individuals have an agreement, whether written or oral, that one party later alleges has been broken, the appropriate action is a breach of contract. There are also claims based not upon an agreement, but on an injury suffered because of the intentional or negligent misconduct of another; this action is a tort. This latter category has been defined as wrongs against the person or property of another, whether intentional or not. It is tort rather than contract that concerns us here.

Torts cover a wide variety of conduct. The most common tort involves the motor vehicle accident, when one person alleges that another drove his car negligently so as to cause a collision and resulting injuries. In order to recover, the claimant (plaintiff) must prove that the other individual (defendant) was negligent, and that the negligence caused the accident that resulted in injuries. In attempting to prove negligence, the plaintiff must establish that the defendant's conduct was unreasonable, i.e., that a reasonable, prudent man would not have acted as he did under the circumstances.

In addition to negligent torts, one may also claim damages by reason of intentional wrongdoing of another. Thus, if a person is involved in a peaceful activity and is struck by another, he has a claim for damages. In addition, the wrongful act may be a crime, but this is a matter for law enforcement officials. We are concerned at this point only in the question of recovering money damages for alleged misconduct. The question arises whether educational institutions may be liable for damages as would an individual.

Educational institutions are generally corporations holding charters from the states in which they are located. As such, they are legal "persons" and are subject to suit for wrongs committed by their agents, including actions for torts. For instance, if a student is struck by a university-operated automobile while standing by the curb, he may claim that the university employee operating the car was negligent. In such a case, the institution will be responsible for the damages if the employee was operating the vehicle as a part of his job duties.

Thus, in general, the educational institution is viewed in the law as a person just as any other corporation is. Accordingly, the actions of its duly authorized agents are attributable to the corporation itself, i.e., the corporation will be liable for the wrongdoing of its employees. The application of this principle to a university setting means that a student may sue the educational institution itself if he suffers injury caused by the negligence of the institution's employees. This, of course, is merely a general statement of a litigant's rights against a university. One should be aware, however, that public universities are generally considered to be agencies of the state; as such, they are immune from suit. This rather strange situation has its origins in the English common law, in which the sovereign was deemed to be above any law but God's and was thus not subject to suit. This medieval principle remains in revised form in most jurisdictions in the United States, but its impact has been blunted by specific statutory provisions. In some states one may secure recovery for negligent acts of state employees by getting a special bill put through the legislature. In others, special tribunals on claims have been created that serve the function of a court in hearing claims